ELIZABETH I

1. *Elizabeth I* in the cloth-of-gold mantle and kirtle she wore at her coronation. This is probably a copy of a lost painting of 1559, by an unknown artist.
(National Portrait Gallery, London)

Elizabeth I

ROSALIND K. MARSHALL

Published in association with
the National Portrait Gallery

London   HMSO

© Rosalind K. Marshall 1991
First published by HMSO 1991

ISBN 0 11 290507 2

Designed by HMSO Graphic Design

British Library Cataloguing in Publication Data
A CIP catalogue record for this book
is available from the British Library

31143007052856
B ELIZABETH I, QUEEN
Marshall, Rosalind Kay.
Elizabeth I

HMSO publications are available from:

HMSO Publications Centre
(Mail and telephone orders only)
PO Box 276, London, SW8 5DT
Telephone orders 071–873 9090
General enquiries 071–873 0011
(queuing system in operation for both numbers)

HMSO Bookshops
49 High Holborn, London, WC1V 6HB   071–873 0011 (Counter service only)
258 Broad Street, Birmingham, B1 2HE   021–643 3740
Southey House, 33 Wine Street, Bristol, BS1 2BQ   0272–264306
9–21 Princess Street, Manchester, M60 8AS   061–834 7201
80 Chichester Street, Belfast, BT1 4JY   0232–238451
71 Lothian Road, Edinburgh, EH3 9AZ   031–228 4181

HMSO's Accredited Agents
(see Yellow Pages)

And through good booksellers

Printed in the United Kingdom for HMSO
Dd 291150   C100   9/91   3735

CONTENTS

2. *Henry VIII*, Elizabeth's father, painted by Hans Holbein about 1536.
(Thyssen-Bornemisza Collection: photograph, Bridgeman Art Library Ltd)

ACKNOWLEDGMENTS

I am grateful to Professor Gordon Donaldson CBE, HM Historiographer in Scotland, who read the completed text of this book for me. I much appreciate the kind assistance and enthusiastic interest of Professor and Mrs C A Mayer (Dana Bentley-Cranch). Gavin Turner, Director of the William Byrd Choir, gave valuable advice on the musical aspects of Elizabeth's reign. I should like to thank Philip Glover and the staff of HMSO for their helpful co-operation, Tess Wright, Dr May Williamson, Diana Scarisbrick, Sarah Wimbush of the Courtauld Institute of Art, Jonathan Franklin of the National Portrait Gallery Archive, and the publications staff of the National Portrait Gallery, London, for their willing assistance with the illustrations.

Spelling and punctuation of sixteenth-century texts have been modernised throughout this book, and French and Latin have been translated into English. Dating is according to the Old Style Julian calendar in use in England throughout Elizabeth's reign.

RKM
Edinburgh, December 1990

ANNA BOLINA VXOR— HENRI' OCTA'

3. *Anne Boleyn*, Elizabeth's mother, by an unknown artist, from a picture of about 1533. (National Portrait Gallery, London)

1

ANNE BOLEYN'S DAUGHTER

O N 22 FEBRUARY 1533 the door to Anne Boleyn's private apartments opened and out she stepped into the crowded hall, a medium-sized woman in her late twenties, with a swarthy complexion, long neck, wide mouth, low bosom and eyes that were black and beautiful. 'The Midnight Crow', her enemy Cardinal Wolsey had called her, and others had even more scurrilous names for her, not without cause. For seven years past King Henry VIII had been infatuated with her and, while his faithful wife Catherine of Aragon watched in horrified disbelief, he pursued this sophisticated, French-educated lady of hers, showering her with gifts and installing her in his palace. Supremely self-confident, with a shrewish temper and an iron will, Anne kept the King dancing attendance on her, refused to sleep with him and laughed at those who dared to criticise her. On her servants' liveries she had emblazoned in French the defiant motto: 'Let them grumble, that is how it is going to be'.

4. *Catherine of Aragon*, Henry VIII's first wife, painted about 1530 by an unknown artist.
(National Portrait Gallery, London)

The question of how it was going to be preoccupied everyone, not just in London but in Paris and Madrid and Rome. Would Henry succeed in putting aside the faithful Catherine, daughter of the late King of Spain, aunt of the Holy Roman Emperor? In spite of all his efforts, he had failed to persuade the Pope to declare his marriage null and void on the grounds that Catherine had been his brother's widow. Would he find some other way of freeing himself from the wife who had given him four stillborn children, a daughter dead in infancy and one surviving child, the Princess Mary? Henry needed sons, for his only boy, the Duke of Richmond, was illegitimate. More than that, he needed Anne, with her quick wit, her sexual allure and her teasing charm. A complete breach with Rome seemed to be the answer. He would become head of the Church of England instead of the Pope.

He was certainly not going to return to his ageing wife. She infuriated him with her patience and her refusal to accept her dismissal. For months she had behaved as though nothing were amiss, sitting in her apartments, sewing shirts for him, maddening him with her dog-like devotion. In the end, irritated beyond endurance, he had sent her away from court and refused to let her see their daughter. Now, it was being said that Madam Anne had at last taken him into her bed. Certainly he had just made her Marchioness of Pembroke and she was more insufferable than ever. Soon, she boasted, very soon, she would be Queen and then she would humble all who had opposed her.

Out she came, into the hall that February day, and glanced around. Noticing a particular friend in the throng, she greeted him in her usual challenging manner and then, well aware that everyone was listening, she called out one of her tantalising remarks. For the last three days, she had had 'such an incredible fierce desire to eat apples as she had never felt before', she said. The King had told her that she must be with child, she went on, but she had said no, it was not so at all. With that, she gave a merry peal of laughter and disappeared back into her apartments again, leaving the courtiers to stare at each other in alarmed speculation.

Could it be true that she was pregnant, or was it another of her peculiar jokes? Only the previous week she had been telling her uncle, the Duke of Norfolk, that if she was not with child by the time Easter came, she would make a pilgrimage to pray to the Virgin Mary. No doubt she was trying to annoy him. She knew that he disapproved of her. Her barbed remarks always had some hidden meaning, however. What was the significance this time? Why had she spoken of a pilgrimage? Everyone knew that she was a Protestant; she would make no pilgrimage. Could she really be pregnant?

She was. Indeed, not only was she expecting the King's child: she was already his wife. As soon as she had told him about her condition he had arranged a quick, secret marriage before dawn, probably in one of the gatehouses at Whitehall Palace. That had been in January, but no announcement could be made until formal arrangements for the break with Rome were complete and Henry could divorce his first wife. Even so, Anne made no attempt to hide her triumph. Two days after the mysterious hints about apples, she was entertaining the King to a lavish banquet in her apartments.

The courtiers noted her air of ill-suppressed excitement, his unusual joviality. Over six feet tall, clad in magnificent garments, he dominated the scene as he always did. In his youth people had marvelled at his fair skin, his auburn hair and his almost girlishly beautiful features. Handsome, athletic, and well-educated, he had seemed the ideal prince. Now, at forty-two, he was heavier, more petulant, and troubled by a varicose ulcer in his leg, but if his subjects quaked at his sudden fierce rages and deplored his marital difficulties, they had lost none of their admiration for his majestic figure and his awe-inspiring presence. Now, as they watched, he leaned over to ask the Duchess of Norfolk what she thought of the beautiful tapestries on the walls and the rich gold plate on the table. All this belonged to her niece Anne, he told her proudly, and smiled at her surprise.

Events moved swiftly after that. Parliament declared that appeals to Rome would now be illegal, the Boleyn family's protégé Thomas Cranmer became Archbishop of Canterbury and Catherine of Aragon was told that she was no longer Queen. In future, she would be known as the Dowager Princess of Wales. On Easter Eve, Anne went with the King to High Mass, wearing a cloth of gold gown 'loaded with the richest jewels' and followed by no fewer than sixty maids of honour. During the service, prayers were said for 'Queen Anne'. Early in May, Cranmer declared that Henry's marriage to Catherine had been invalid from the start and at the end of the month his new bride was crowned, with pageants, processions and feasting.

5. *Thomas Cranmer, Archbishop of Canterbury*, Elizabeth's godfather, painted in 1546 by Gerlach Flicke.
(National Portrait Gallery, London)

6. *Thomas Howard, 3rd Duke of Norfolk*, uncle of Anne Boleyn and Katherine Howard, 1538–9.
(Reproduced by gracious permission of Her Majesty The Queen)

7. *Greenwich from the park, showing the Tudor Palace,* painted about 1620 by an unknown artist.
(The Trustees of the National Maritime Museum)

By this time Anne was six months pregnant, and she was making plans for her confinement. To please her, the King gave orders for a particularly elaborate bed to be taken from his treasure room and installed at Greenwich Palace. It had once been part of the ransom of a French prince. She then demanded the exquisite christening robe which Catherine of Aragon had brought from Spain for her own children. Henry obediently told Catherine to hand it over. She refused and so he had another even grander one made, to console his bride for the disappointment.

Anne was always ready to take him to task when he displeased her, and that summer there was an ugly scene when she accused him of paying too much attention to one of the ladies of the court. He lost his temper, retorting that she must shut her eyes and endure, as those who were better than she had done. In spite of this wounding reference to his first wife, they soon made up their quarrel, and at the end of the summer when Anne fell ill he was desperately worried. However, the astrologers he consulted assured him that she would have a safe labour and, better still, that she would bear him a living son.

While he organised a lavish celebratory tournament and his goldsmith worked on a silver cradle set with jewels, designed by the court artist Hans Holbein, Anne's clerks wrote out letters announcing the birth of the Prince. At the end of August, she took up residence in the chambers prepared for her in Greenwich Palace, and on 7 September 1533, between three and four in the afternoon, her child was born. The astrologers had been right in one of their predictions. Anne's labour was easy and she recovered rapidly. They were wrong in their other prognostication. The baby was a girl.

While bells rang out over London, the clerks hastily amended the birth announcement and the King cancelled the tournament. Bonfires were lit that night and a solemn *Te Deum* was sung in St Paul's Cathedral the following day, but it was Henry's Roman Catholic adversaries who really rejoiced, gratified as they were at the King of England's discomfiture and this unexpected reversal in the fortunes of 'the Concubine'. Highly-coloured rumours circulated round Europe claiming that Anne had given birth to a monster, that her child was dead or that Henry intended calling his newly-born bastard Mary, as a calculated insult to his legitimate daughter.

In fact, there is no evidence about his true feelings. He had every reason to suppose that next time Anne would present him with his prince, but of course he must have been disappointed and he did not attend the baby's christening. The ceremony took place in the Friary Church at Greenwich on Wednesday of that same week and, the King's absence apart, it was as splendid as Anne could have desired.

The procession set off from Greenwich Palace, led by citizens of London, gentlemen, esquires, chaplains, the aldermen in scarlet robes and the Lord Mayor in his crimson velvet gown. The King's Council followed, with the royal chaplains, the bishops and the peers of the realm. Next came those courtiers who had been selected to carry the items to be used in the baptism. The old Earl of Essex had the gilt basins, the Marquess of Exeter bore a large taper of virgin wax and the Marquess of Dorset was in charge of the magnificent salt which would be used to purify the infant.

Spectators, crushed together in front of the tapestry-hung buildings lining the route, waited impatiently for the most important part of the procession. At last, the Duchess of Norfolk came into view; on her right, her husband, with his Marshal's rod of office, and on her left, the Duke of Suffolk, brother-

in-law of the King. In her arms she bore the sumptuous new christening robe sewn with pearls and precious stones.

Behind her, bobbing about over the heads of the dignitaries, was a rich canopy, held aloft by Anne Boleyn's brother and three more of her kinsmen, and under the canopy was the Dowager Duchess of Norfolk, with the three-day-old baby in her arms. The infant was wrapped in a purple velvet mantle with an ermine-lined train so long and so heavy that Anne's father and one of his friends had to walk along on either side to support it, while the Countess of Kent held up the hem. Behind them came crowds of ladies and gentle-women, hurrying along the streets strewn with fresh green rushes, anxious not to miss a moment of the ceremonial.

By the time the baby arrived at the church door, the Bishop of London was waiting to greet her, flanked by fellow bishops and abbots. Inside, everything was ready. The walls were hung with fine tapestries, and a silver font had been placed on a raised platform beneath a crimson satin canopy fringed with gold. Various notabilities wearing aprons hovered anxiously nearby to make sure that no mud or dirt soiled the carpet.

A fire was flickering in a special pan set between the choir and the nave, and there the infant was put into her christening robe. She was then carried to the font, to be baptised by the Bishop of London. Her godfather was Thomas Cranmer, Archbishop of Canterbury, and her godmothers were the old Duchess of Norfolk and the Dowager Marchioness of Dorset. As soon as it was done, Garter King of Arms stepped forward to proclaim in a loud voice, 'God of his infinite goodness send prosperous life and long to the high and mighty Princess of England, Elizabeth!' She was not to be called Mary, after all. Henry had chosen for her his own mother's name, deliberately emphasis-ing that this was his legitimate daughter, a true member of the royal Tudor dynasty, descendant of the houses of both York and Lancaster.

As soon as she had been christened, the Princess Elizabeth was carried to the altar to be confirmed by the Archbishop of Canterbury, and then her godparents presented her with gifts. There was a standing gold cup from

Cranmer, a cup set with pearls from the Dowager Duchess of Norfolk and three gilt bowls from Lady Exeter. That done, everyone relaxed, and refreshments were brought in: wafers, confections and cups of wine flavoured with spices. Suitably fortified, the procession formed up again, with trumpeters leading the way and the christening gifts proudly displayed by specially chosen bearers.

The service had been a long one and it was dark now, so on each side of the procession guards and servants walked with torches, at least five hundred of them, while the gentlemen round about the baby carried many more. Princess Elizabeth was brought back to the door of her mother's apartments and handed carefully to her nurses, while the Mayor and the aldermen were taken down to the cellars for a drink, on the King's personal instructions.

Elizabeth spent her first weeks in the royal nurseries, tended by her wet-nurse, her dry-nurses, the women who rocked her cradle and the women who did her laundry. When she was three months old, she was given her own household, as etiquette required, and on a cold, mid-December afternoon she was carried out to a richly decorated litter and taken in procession through the streets of London, escorted by her great-uncle, the Duke of Norfolk. They stopped at Lord Rutland's house in Enfield for the night, and next morning they went on to the palace of Hatfield, in Hertfordshire, which was to be her home.

As soon as he had seen the baby safely settled in her crimson satin cradle, the Duke rode off to Essex on an embarrassing mission. He was to fetch Princess Mary. Already deprived of her title of Princess of Wales and told that

9. *A Young Lady, probably Elizabeth's sister Mary*, drawn by Hans Holbein about 1536. (Windsor Castle, Royal Library. © Her Majesty The Queen)

10. The Old Palace of Hatfield, Elizabeth's childhood home.
(Photograph, A F Kersting)

she was illegitimate, the resentful seventeen-year-old was to go to Hatfield as one of her half-sister's ladies in waiting. When he told her, she raged and wept. It was a deliberate humiliation, devised, no doubt, by Anne Boleyn. Throughout her parents' marital problems Mary had staunchly supported her mother, but in spite of everything she still idolised her father, blaming all their troubles on 'the Concubine'. When Norfolk unwisely referred to Elizabeth as 'Princess of Wales', Mary drew herself up and told him proudly, 'That is a title which belongs to me by right and no one else'. He growled that he was there not to argue but to see his King's wishes accomplished, and in the end she had to go with him.

Now, instead of presiding over her own household of sympathetic Roman Catholic retainers, she was surrounded by Protestant Howards and Boleyns, and as if that were not mortification enough, a stream of insulting messages came from the so-called Queen. Anne told the steward's wife to give Mary a box on the ears from time to time, 'for being the cursed bastard she is'. The girl's life became a constant battle to assert what she believed to be her own rightful inheritance.

Mary's unhappiness and her obstinacy were disturbing elements in Elizabeth's early childhood. Whenever the household moved to a different location, there was another embarrassing scene. They did not stay at Hatfield all the year round. The inadequacies of Tudor sanitation meant that a palace had to be cleansed thoroughly every few months, and so they would move to Hunsdon or Ashridge or the More, or to one of the royal palaces. Whatever the destination, the procedure was the same. Mary defiantly refused to take second place in any travelling arrangements. Once, she even had to be dragged out forcibly by the gentlemen of the household and thrown into her litter. Her friend the Imperial ambassador urged her not to repeat such an undignified spectacle and so after that she concentrated on racing out first so that she could snatch the place of honour in the procession for herself.

These dramas apart, life in the household was carefully regulated. All major decisions had to be referred to the King, and so when Lady Bryan decided that Elizabeth, at two, was old enough to be weaned, his permission had to be sought before the wet-nurse could be put away. Anne too kept a close watch on the nursery. She chose all Elizabeth's clothes. She had excellent taste, and her own outfits were always elegant and in the height of French fashion. Now her personal tailor, William Loke, made Elizabeth's garments also. The child was like her father in colouring, with golden-red hair and a very fair skin, and Anne ordered dresses of white damask, green satin and yellow satin for her, with detachable embroidered sleeves in crimson, purple and white. Over that, she wore velvet coats of black, russet and orange, and on her head went caps in regal purple satin trimmed with gold. These details mattered, for clothing was an important indication of status.

Wherever their daughter might be, Henry and Anne paid regular visits, commenting enthusiastically on Elizabeth's appearance and steadfastly ignoring Mary. Until she recognised him as Supreme Head of the Church of England, the King would have nothing to do with her. It was vital to him that she should submit, for if she did not, she might become a rallying-point for other discontented Roman Catholics. He had already sent his former Lord Chancellor, Sir Thomas More, to the block for refusing to comply. Mary might well be next.

In March 1534, parliament passed an Act of Succession declaring that his offspring by Anne were his only lawful heirs. Henry did not have Elizabeth in mind, of course, when he devised this piece of legislation. His wife would surely do her duty soon and present him with sons. The sexual attraction between them was as strong as ever and he was fascinated by her energy and her assertiveness. She shared his love of music, patronised artists like Holbein and protected her radical Protestant friends, but he had to admit that she was not the easiest companion. If she was not complaining that she could not sleep for the squawking of his peacocks she was ranting about his fondness for Mary or nagging him about the attentions he paid to colourless little Jane Seymour and the other ladies of the court. Sometimes he found himself thinking nostalgically of Catherine's tranquil company. She had never bullied him or made strange jokes or given vent to wild bursts of disconcerting laughter. Life with Anne was exciting, but it was not comfortable.

She did not become pregnant again until Elizabeth was two years old, although she may have had one or two miscarriages before that. Henry was triumphant, and that winter brought them further exciting news. On 8 January 1536, Catherine of Aragon died of cancer at Kimbolton Castle. 'Thank God!' cried Henry, when he was told. 'We are now free from any fear of war!' Catherine's nephew, the Emperor Charles V, would no longer threaten to come to her rescue with his armies.

Henry and Anne had been at Greenwich for Christmas, and Charles's ambassador, Eustace Chapuys, noted that on the following day the King appeared 'dressed entirely in yellow from head to foot, with the single exception of a white feather in his cap'. Princess Elizabeth was there too. It was Sunday, and that morning she was taken to church 'to the sound of trumpets

11. *Charles V*, Holy Roman Emperor and nephew of Catherine of Aragon, by Titian.
(Kunsthistorisches Museum, Vienna)

and with great display'. After dinner, Henry went down to the hall where the ladies of the court were dancing, and there he 'made great demonstrations of joy, and at last went to his own apartments, took the little bastard [Elizabeth] in his arms, and began to show her first to one, then to another, and did the same the following day'.

Catherine was buried in Peterborough Cathedral on 29 January, and that same day Anne had a miscarriage. The baby would have been a boy. Henry was bitterly disappointed. 'I see that God will not give me male children', he told his wife as she lay in bed recovering and then, with a curt 'When you are up I will speak to you', he turned on his heel and went out. Anne consoled herself by blaming the Duke of Norfolk for the whole unhappy episode. If he had not come bursting into her apartments to announce that Henry had suffered a fall at tilting, she might yet have been carrying her royal son, she said.

The King, for his part, remained morbidly obsessed with the thought that he was the victim of divine retribution. He had not married his brother's wife this time, it was true, but he was convinced that Anne had lured him into marriage by means of witchcraft. Deciding that he would never have his prince until he found a different wife, he consulted Bishop Stokesley of London about the best way to obtain another divorce. Pale, fair-haired Jane Seymour

10

might not have Anne's vivacity or her sex appeal, but she would make a restful companion after all the domestic turmoil he had recently endured. He would marry her instead.

Horrified, the Bishop refused to commit himself and so Henry turned to his own secretary, Thomas Cromwell. He had been useful in making possible the marriage with Anne. Now he could find a means of getting rid of her. Cromwell obediently went to work and on 2 May 1536, the Queen was arrested on charges of adultery and treason. Sobbing and laughing hysterically, she was sent to the Tower. At her trial on 15 May she was in command of herself again, denying with dignity the charge that she had taken lovers: Sir Henry Norris, Gentleman of her Privy Chamber, William Brereton and Sir Francis Weston of her household, Mark Smeaton her young lute player and her own brother George, Viscount Rochford. With them, she was alleged to have plotted the death of the King.

Norris, Brereton, Weston and Smeaton had been convicted the previous day. Now, in the Great Hall of the Tower, before their uncle the Duke of Norfolk who was in charge of the proceedings, Anne and her brother were found guilty. Weeping, Norfolk sentenced them both to death. Rochford, Norris, Smeaton, Weston and Brereton were executed two days later. On 17 May, Anne's marriage to Henry was pronounced null and void. She should have died the following day, but the King had granted her request that she should be executed by a swordsman, in the French fashion, rather than on the block, and a special executioner was having to be brought over from Calais.

12. *Thomas Cromwell*, Secretary of Henry VIII, painted by
an unknown artist from a portrait by Holbein.
(National Portrait Gallery, London)

EARL OF ESSEX.

13. Tower Green, where Anne Boleyn was executed.
(Photograph, James Bartholomew)

14. The Chapel of St Peter-ad-Vincula, where Anne Boleyn was buried.
(Photograph, James Bartholomew)

As she waited, she seemed to be in a mood of strange exaltation, alternating between hopes of release and the desire to have her troubles ended. 'I heard say the executioner was very good, and I have a little neck', she remarked to the Constable of the Tower, and 'put her hands about it, laughing heartily'. 'I have seen many men and also women executed', the Constable commented, 'and all they have been in great sorrow, and to my knowledge this lady has much joy and pleasure in death'.

She was taken to Tower Green at about eight o'clock the following morning, her fur-lined gown of grey damask and her red skirt concealed by an ermine-trimmed mantle, her black hair hidden by her headdress. A Spaniard living in London at the time was there, and it seemed to him that she was 'as gay as if she was not going to die'. She took off her mantle, changed her headdress for a cap and said a few last words. The swordsman stepped forward when she was looking the other way and in seconds she was dead. Her ladies wrapped her body in a sheet and carried it to the chapel of St Peter-ad-Vincula in the Tower. There she was buried, in an elm chest meant to contain bows.

No one knows who told Elizabeth what had happened, or what she felt. She was very young, not yet three, but she must have been aware of the excitement around her, the weeping of the women and the fact that her mother had gone away. As soon as Henry VIII heard that his wife had been executed, he set off to visit Jane Seymour. They were betrothed the following day and on 30 May he married her.

Elizabeth's whole household was thrown into a state of disarray. Henry was preoccupied with his new wife and now that Anne Boleyn was gone there was no one to give the necessary orders about the child's clothing. Before long, Lady Bryan was having to complain that her charge 'hath neither gown nor kirtle nor petticoat nor no manner of linen nor smocks nor kerchiefs nor rails nor body stitchets nor handkerchiefs nor sleeves nor mufflers nor biggins [caps]'.

To make matters worse, John Shelton, her mother's uncle, was disrupting the daily routine by impudently insisting that Elizabeth should take her meals with everyone else in the hall instead of eating in her own nursery quarters. Much upset by this interference, Lady Bryan wrote to protest to the King. If his daughter were brought to the general table, 'she shall see divers meats and fruits and wine which it would be hard for me to restrain Her Grace' from eating. She was anxious not to treat the little girl harshly, for she was teething, and in great discomfort. It would be difficult to punish her if she did misbehave, for there was no place of correction at Hatfield where she could be shut away until she mended her ways and 'she is yet too young to correct greatly'. She was, however, Lady Bryan concluded proudly, 'as toward [forward] a child, and as gentle of condition, as ever I knew in my life'.

The exact date of the letter is not known, but at the end of June the King gave orders for Elizabeth's household to be reorganised, allowing her thirty-two servants. Her sister was not one of them. After months of wretched defiance and ill-health, Mary had finally submitted to the King. She had signed a humiliating document recognising him as Supreme Head of the Church of England, renouncing her allegiance to the Pope and even acknowledging that her mother's marriage to her father had been unlawful. She regretted her surrender almost at once, torturing herself for the rest of her life with the thought that she had betrayed her mother, but her situation did improve rapidly as a result. Suddenly she was the King's beloved daughter again, brought back to court for an affectionate reunion and kindly received by the

15. *Jane Seymour*, Elizabeth's first stepmother, by Holbein. (Windsor Castle, Royal Library. © 1990 Her Majesty The Queen)

stepmother who was just six years older than herself.

Jane was pregnant by this time and parliament had passed a new Act of Succession declaring that the children of this marriage would be Henry's heirs: like Mary, Elizabeth was now regarded as being illegitimate. When Lady Bryan's husband told the child that in future she would no longer have her royal title, she stared at him unwinkingly and retorted, 'How haps it, Governor, yesterday my Lady Princess, and today but my Lady Elizabeth?' He could give no suitable reply.

Jane was eager to gather her new family together, and so both Elizabeth and Mary were summoned to Hampton Court for her confinement. At two o'clock in the morning, on 12 October 1537, her son was born and Henry was triumphant. After all the fears, the disappointments and the tragedies of the past, he finally had his prince. Three days later, Elizabeth attended the christening in the palace chapel. She was in charge of the baptismal robe. It was too heavy for her to carry, of course, and so she was borne along in the arms of Jane's brother Edward, Earl of Hertford.

Mary was godmother and another Seymour brother, Thomas, helped to support the canopy of state. The infant was christened Edward and, when the service was over, Elizabeth marched out of the chapel holding Mary's hand. It seemed that a new era of domestic happiness for the royal family had begun, but on 24 October Queen Jane died of puerperal sepsis. She was buried at Windsor in November and Elizabeth returned to her own household.

2

THE LADY ELIZABETH

W*HILE HENRY* sank into self-pitying gloom, Elizabeth resumed her accustomed way of life in the country, occasionally meeting Mary or Edward and sometimes spending a few weeks at court. At first, the King was very much the melancholy widower, but he knew that he must marry again sooner or later and in 1540 Elizabeth arrived to find a startling change in his ménage. By his side was a plain, ingenuous-looking foreign lady who spoke no English but smiled delightedly at everyone. This, Elizabeth was told, was her father's new wife, Anne of Cleves. Sister of a German Lutheran duke, Anne neither danced, sang nor played an instrument. Instead, she sat sewing for most of the time, apparently oblivious to her husband's dark looks.

Henry felt cheated. He had been told that the lady was chaste and obedient, and he had been pleased with her portrait, but as soon as he had laid eyes on her he had been seized by a violent dislike and he felt quite unable to consummate their marriage. He divorced her as quickly as he could, but she did not disappear from the scene. Relieved to return to spinsterhood, she lived on happily in England, enjoying the position of a kind of honorary aunt to the royal family. Elizabeth liked her, and they used to ride together in processions whenever there was an important state occasion.

Henry did not intend to remain single, of course. Not only did he need more sons: he was passionately in love again. A new lady had appeared at court and she had taken his eye at once, for she bore a striking resemblance to Anne Boleyn. Dark, pretty Katherine Howard was Anne's first cousin, and she had the same vivacity and allure. As soon as he was free, Henry married her. Elizabeth was given a place of honour at the wedding banquet and in May 1541 she spent a few days with the Queen at Chelsea. The following winter, however, Katherine suddenly disappeared. Henry had discovered that she was promiscuous. She had not even been a virgin when he married her. He sent her to the Tower and on 13 February 1543 she was beheaded. She was buried near her cousin in the Chapel of St Peter-ad-Vincula.

Elizabeth was eight now, a sharp, intelligent child who must have heard some of the gossip, some of the whispered references to her own mother's fate. Her precocity was well-known. She was 'as grave as a woman of forty', the King's secretary had reported with amusement when he met her two years earlier. She knew how to behave in processions and at state ceremonies, she could sew beautiful cambric shirts for her small brother and she could read and write. Already her governess Kate Champernowne was introducing her to Latin and Greek. She and Kate, a well-educated young woman from Devon, were great friends and the other members of her establishment were trusted allies too. Lady Bryan had gone to be governess to Prince Edward but Elizabeth still had Blanche Parry, who had rocked her in her cradle, Thomas Parry, her plump Welsh treasurer, and John Ashley, her faithful gentleman.

Fond as she was of them, they were no substitute for relatives. Her relationship with them was always that of mistress and servant. She was the King's daughter and neither she nor they forgot it. Surrounded though she was by these familiar companions, she was in many ways emotionally isolated and forced into self-reliance. The King was a magnificent figure to be worshipped

15

16. *Anne of Cleves*, Elizabeth's second stepmother, a miniature painted by a follower of Holbein.
(By courtesy of the Board of Trustees of the Victoria and Albert Museum)

from afar, rather than a loving parent, and the stepmothers who came and went were really only inferiors whom he had chosen to favour for the time being, as long as they behaved themselves.

Henry's sixth and final wife was, however, to be an important influence in all their lives. After the dramatic ending of his union with Katherine Howard,

17. *Katherine Howard*, Elizabeth's third stepmother, by an unknown artist (National Portrait Gallery, London)

Henry turned for comfort to a lady long known to him. Katherine Parr was the sister of his reliable friend the Marquess of Northampton. She had been brought up at court; indeed, she had been educated with Mary. Thirty-one years old now, Katherine had auburn hair, a round, doll-like face and a firm little mouth. She had been married twice already, both times to much older men, and she had been twice widowed. She did not want to marry the King, because she was deeply in love with Jane Seymour's brother Thomas, but she dared not refuse. Abandoning all hope of having a husband of her own choice, she married Henry in the Queen's Privy Chamber at Hampton Court on 12 July 1543.

Elizabeth, Edward and her old friend Mary were at the wedding and, childless herself, Katherine decided to take a special interest in her new family. A devout, cultivated Protestant, she was anxious that they should have a

18. *Katherine Parr*, Elizabeth's fourth and final stepmother, painted by an unknown artist about 1545.
(National Portrait Gallery, London)

19. *Sir John Cheke*, tutor of Edward VI.
This is a cast of a medal which was
possibly struck in Italy in 1555.
(National Portrait Gallery, London)

suitable education and she encouraged Henry to lure a clutch of eminent
Protestant scholars from Oxford and Cambridge to teach the Prince. Whenever
Elizabeth was in the same house, she shared his lessons, and so she too
studied with Dr Richard Cox, the headmaster of Eton, John Cheke, Professor
of Greek, Sir Anthony Coke and the bluff young Roger Ascham. Apart from
the classics, she read French and Italian with her brother's masters, Jean
Belmain and Battista Castiglione.

Elizabeth had a quick, retentive mind and, taught by such austere, learned
gentlemen, both she and Edward developed a highly elaborate prose style
and a prematurely adult outlook on life. 'Unkind fortune, envious of all good
and the continuous whirl of human affairs has deprived me for a whole year
of your most illustrious presence . . .', she was writing at ten years old, in
Italian, to her stepmother. '. . . I understand that your most Illustrious Highness has not forgotten me every time you have written to the King's Majesty,
which it was my duty to have requested from you, since I have not dared to
write to him myself. I now humbly beseech your most Excellent Highness
that when you write to His Majesty you will recommend me to him, praying
always for his sweet blessing and similarly entreating our Lord God to send
him best success and the obtaining of victory over his enemies . . .'

Henry was away in France at the time, trying to capture Boulogne, and
Katherine was acting as Regent. The King came back triumphant at Christmas
1544, and Elizabeth, staying at Ashridge with Edward, busied herself making
a very special present for Katherine. She carefully copied out a translation of
a long religious poem by the French King's sister entitled *The Mirror of the Sinful
Soul*, made a cover embroidered with a design incorporating her stepmother's
initials, and presented it to her as a New Year's gift.

By now, Elizabeth had her own tutor, a young Cambridge scholar named
William Grindal, and under his influence she worked so hard at her books
that Roger Ascham, who had maintained a friendly interest in her, felt that
he must intervene. He sent a letter of advice to Kate Champernowne, now
married to her fellow-servant John Ashley, declaring that his own preferred
regime of more relaxed studies would benefit Elizabeth. 'Blunt edges be dull
and endure much pain to little profit', he observed, but 'the free edge is soon
turned if it be not handled thereafter. If you pour much drink at once into a
goblet, the most part will dash out and run over. If ye pour it softly, you may
fill it even to the top, and so Her Grace, I doubt not, by little and little may
be increased in learning . . . I send My Lady her pen, an Italian book, a book

20. *The Family of Henry VIII*, by an unknown artist, about 1545. This contains the earliest portrait of Elizabeth, on the right. Jane Seymour, although dead, is next to the King, with Edward and Mary on the left. In the background is the Great Garden at Whitehall. (Reproduced by gracious permission of Her Majesty The Queen)

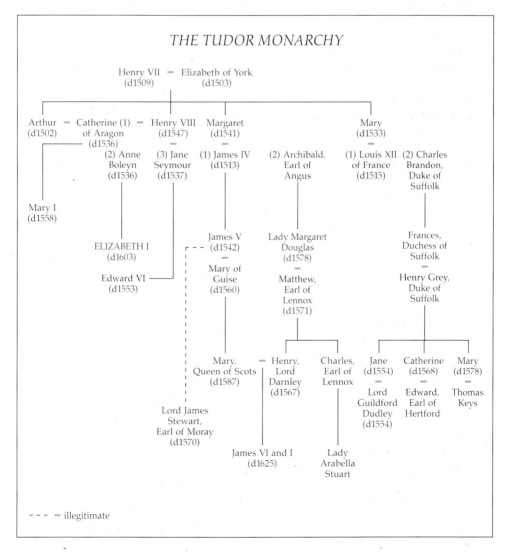

THE TUDOR MONARCHY

Henry VII = Elizabeth of York
(d1509) (d1503)

Arthur = Catherine (1) = Henry VIII   Margaret   Mary
(d1502)   of Aragon   (d1547)   (d1541)   (d1533)
          (d1536)   =   =
          (2) Anne   (3) Jane   (1) James IV   (2) Archibald,   (1) Louis XII (2) Charles
          Boleyn   Seymour   (d1513)   Earl of   of France   Brandon,
          (d1536)   (d1537)   Angus   (d1515)   Duke of
                                                                                    Suffolk

Mary I
(d1558)

                                        James V   Lady Margaret   Frances,
          ELIZABETH I   (d1542)   Douglas   Duchess of
          (d1603)   =   (d1578)   Suffolk
                                        Mary of   =
          Edward VI   Guise   Matthew,   Henry Grey,
          (d1553)   (d1560)   Earl of   Duke of
                                                        Lennox   Suffolk
                                                        (d1571)

                            Mary,   = Henry,   Charles,   Jane   Catherine   Mary
                            Queen of Scots Lord   Earl of   (d1554)   (d1568)   (d1578)
                            (d1587)   Darnley   Lennox   =   =   =
                                         (d1567)   Lord   Edward,   Thomas
          Lord James   Guildford   Earl of   Keys
          Stewart,   Dudley   Hertford
          Earl of Moray   (d1554)
          (d1570)
                            James VI and I   Lady
                            (d1625)   Arabella
                                                   Stuart

- - - = illegitimate

of prayers. Send the silver pen which is broken, and it shall be mended quickly.'

Regardless of Ascham's advice, Elizabeth continued her long hours of study. She had soon learned that her aptitude for the classics brought her approbation and attention, and by the end of that year she was compiling another gift, this time for the King himself. Queen Katherine had published a modest devotional work entitled *Prayers and Meditations*. Elizabeth translated it into Latin, French and Italian and embroidered a beautiful red cover with gold and silver.

She sent it to him from Hertford Castle in December 1545, with an elegant Latin letter urging him to overlook any errors in it 'on account of my ignorance, my youth, my short time of study and my goodwill, and if it be undistinguished, even though it merit no praise, yet if it be well received it will powerfully incite me to further efforts so that even as I advance in years so

21. *Elizabeth*, aged about thirteen, by an unknown artist.
(Reproduced by gracious permission of Her Majesty The Queen)

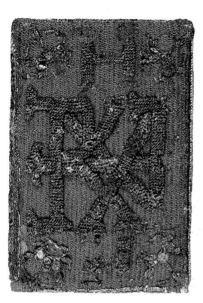

22. The cover of the prayer book embroidered by Elizabeth for her father in 1545.
(The British Library)

23. *Prince Edward*, painted for his father in about 1546, by an unknown artist.
(Reproduced by gracious permission of Her Majesty The Queen)

shall I advance also in learning and in the fear of God, and so it shall come to pass that I shall worship Him ever more zealously and serve Your Majesty ever more dutifully'. There was not, nor could there be, anything spontaneous in Elizabeth's relationship with her father.

By this time, Henry was ageing rapidly and in reality he was very different from the magnificent, benevolent, idealised monarch of his daughter's imagining. Grossly overweight, uncertain of temper and suffering from life-threatening blood clots in his bad leg, he fell victim to a series of violent fevers. Several times in 1546 he alarmed his retinue with near-fatal collapses and when he took ill again in January 1547 he failed to recover. Elizabeth was staying at Enfield when she was surprised by the sudden arrival of her brother, accompanied by his Seymour uncle Edward, Earl of Hertford. A tall, imposing man with a long fair beard, Hertford broke the news to them together. The King had died in the early hours of 28 January. The nine-year-old Prince was now King Edward VI of England. Frightened, both children burst into tears.

The following day, Edward was taken away to London. He was far too young to rule for himself, of course, and his father had left a will appointing a Council of Regency. As his uncle, Hertford was in a particularly advantageous position, and he quickly seized power, declaring himself Lord Protector of England. Mary's and Elizabeth's futures were secured by a clause in their father's will which stipulated that if anything should happen to Edward, the crown would pass to Mary, and if she too died childless, then Elizabeth would succeed.

While the Lord Protector accumulated for himself a series of imposing titles including that of Duke of Somerset, the widowed Queen Katherine retired to Chelsea Palace, her own pleasant, red-brick house by the Thames. It was agreed that Elizabeth should go to stay with her, but if the Lord Protector imagined that she would lead a quiet, uneventful life there, dividing her time between her studies and her devotions, he had reckoned without the intervention of his own brother, Thomas Seymour.

24. *Thomas Seymour*, brother of Jane Seymour and husband of Katherine Parr, by an unknown artist.
(National Portrait Gallery, London)

'Nearly forty now and Lord High Admiral of England, Thomas was tall, handsome and full of boisterous good humour. Beneath the outward bonhomie, however, lay a rash, ambitious nature. He was bitterly jealous of his elder brother and he resolved that, somehow or other, he would oust him. For a week or two he toyed with the idea of marrying the Lady Elizabeth, but a far greater prize was within his grasp. Katherine Parr was obviously still in love with him, and just four months after Henry VIII's death, he married her.

He moved in with her at once, and the doleful atmosphere of a mourning household was immediately transformed by the lighthearted gaiety of the newlyweds. Lord Protector Somerset was furious, it was true, but there was nothing that either he or his unpleasant wife could do about it. Thomas was full of exciting schemes, financial and dynastic, one of them involving Lady Jane Grey, daughter of a cousin of Elizabeth. She could be an extremely useful pawn in his complicated game. He bribed her father to let her come to Chelsea Palace as his ward and a few weeks later she arrived, with her tutor and her books.

A serious, scholarly girl with a strong will beneath her apparent timidity, Jane had been unhappy at home with her unsympathetic parents and she was probably glad enough to be taken into kindhearted Katherine's care. Elizabeth's reaction to her is not recorded, but Jane presumably merged quietly into the background. She would certainly not have responded with Elizabeth's animation to Lord Thomas's fast and furious teasing.

When he got up in the morning, he marched into Elizabeth's bedchamber to wish her a hearty good day, slapped her on the buttocks and then strode off to bother her maids of honour with his nonsense. If she was not yet up, he had even greater fun. He stamped over to the bed, pulled open its curtains and made as if to pounce on the occupant, while she shrieked and giggled and burrowed under the clothes for protection. Mrs Ashley slept with Elizabeth and so she was always present, but she liked Thomas and her occasional rebukes were halfhearted.

Katherine accepted all this as part of her husband's jovial good nature, and when they moved to Hanworth in Middlesex, one of her country houses, she joined in the fun. She came with him to Elizabeth's chamber in the morning to tickle her mercilessly as she lay in bed and once, when they were romping together in the gardens, she held her stepdaughter while Thomas cut the girl's dress into strips, roaring with laughter at her rage and her struggles.

Such boisterous antics attracted attention, of course, and Mrs Ashley's husband began to worry that the situation was getting out of hand. He could see that Elizabeth's feelings were involved, 'that the Lady Elizabeth did bear some affection to My Lord Admiral', for 'sometimes she would blush when he were spoken of'. A vulnerable adolescent, she could easily be hurt, but there was more to worry about than that. As the King's sister, she must be carefully guarded, for if there were any hint of impropriety, then they would all be in trouble. Mrs Ashley brushed his warnings aside, but she did tell Lord Thomas that it was unseemly for him to come to her charge's chamber in his dressing-gown and although he blustered as usual, he stopped doing it.

Even so, matters did not end there. One day, Katherine glanced in at the window of the long gallery just in time to see Elizabeth fling her arms about the Lord Admiral's neck and kiss him enthusiastically. Horrified, the Queen Dowager decided that Elizabeth could no longer remain in her household. The girl's departure would have to be accomplished with discretion, for if she left too suddenly it would simply draw attention to her. She could go at first

25. *Kate Ashley*, Elizabeth's governess, by an unknown artist.
(The Lord Hastings)

26. *John Ashley*, Kate's husband, by an unknown artist.
(The Lord Hastings)

to Cheshunt, where she often stayed with Sir Anthony and Lady Denny, and then she could move back to Hatfield. If anyone expressed surprise, Katherine's own health could be given as the excuse. At the age of thirty-five she was pregnant for the first time, and she could say that she needed rest and quiet.

Elizabeth said little when Katherine explained it to her, emphasising the need for a king's daughter to guard her reputation. Thomas's attentions had been delightful fun after her sober, somewhat solitary existence and she had for the first time enjoyed the experience of flirting with an attractive older man.

Guiltily aware that her behaviour had been not quite as it should have been, she worried at first that she might have forfeited Katherine's favour, but soon there were kind letters from her stepmother and she saw that all was well. The two of them corresponded, mentioning Thomas from time to time in natural terms, and Elizabeth joked about the coming baby. If she were at his birth, she said, 'no doubt I would see him beaten for the trouble he hath put you to' – an allusion to the custom of slapping a newborn infant to start his breathing.

There was no question of Elizabeth being there, of course, although Jane Grey accompanied Katherine and Thomas to Sudeley Castle in Gloucestershire that summer. There, on 30 August 1548, Katherine gave birth to a girl whom she named Mary, after her elder stepdaughter. At first she seemed to be recovering well from labour, but then her temperature soared and she fell into delirium. Her ladies nursed her devotedly, Thomas lay down on the bed beside her to try to quieten her, but it was no use. She died five days later of puerperal fever. Most accounts say that her child died in infancy, but at least one nineteenth-century historian was convinced that little Mary grew up, married and had descendants who were still alive in that writer's own day.

When news of Katherine's death reached Ashridge, where Elizabeth was staying, Kate Ashley's reaction was swift and to the point. 'Now he is free again!' she exclaimed joyfully. Elizabeth said nothing, but she blushed deeply. The same thought had crossed Thomas's own mind for all his genuine grief, and at the end of the year he made his move. He knew that Elizabeth had no London residence because Durham House, which should have been hers, was being used as a Mint, so he offered her his own mansion, Seymour Place, fully furnished. He promised to do all he could to expedite the formalities needed to put her into possession of other lands left to her by her father, and he suggested exchanging certain properties with her in order to regularise her estate boundaries. Elizabeth made noncommittal replies.

27. Katherine Parr's room at Sudeley Castle, Gloucestershire.
(Photograph, A F Kersting)

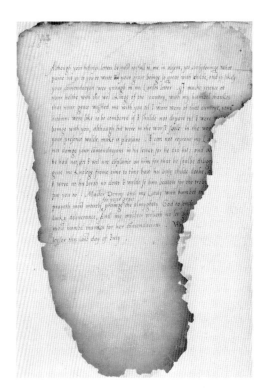

28. Letter from Elizabeth to Katherine Parr, joking that if she were at the birth of Katherine's hoped-for son, 'no doubt I would see him beaten for the trouble [he] put you to'. (The British Library)

Her retinue, meanwhile, waited with bated breath to see what would happen next. They were convinced that he was doing all this because he meant to marry her. She would need the consent of the Lord Protector and the Council of Regency, of course, but Thomas was so enterprising he could surely obtain even that. They had no doubts about Elizabeth's own attitude: Parry noticed how her face lit up whenever Thomas Seymour was mentioned, especially if he were being praised.

Eager to find out if there had been any fresh developments, Parry teased Mrs Ashley one evening by declaring that Lord Thomas was greedy, evil and had been a bad husband to Katherine Parr. Mrs Ashley leaped to the Lord Admiral's defence, just as Parry had known she would. 'Tush, tush!' she exclaimed, 'that is no matter. I know him better than ye do, or those that so report him. I know he will make but too much of her, and that she knows well enough!'

Christmas came and went and there was no news until suddenly, in mid-January, a group of horsemen rode up to the gates of Hatfield Palace, where Elizabeth was staying. As soon as he saw the men coming, Thomas Parry, white-faced, bolted up to his room to tell his wife, 'I would I had never been born, for I am undone', and in his despair he 'wrung his hands, and cast away his chain from his neck and his rings from his fingers'.

It was small wonder he was afraid. The visitors had come to interrogate the household. Lord Thomas Seymour was a prisoner in the Tower of London, they said, charged with high treason. He had been found conspiring to over-throw the Lord Protector. He had intended marrying off Jane Grey to Edward and then taking Elizabeth as his own wife, so that he could rule England as Regent on behalf of the young King. Parry and the Ashleys were questioned, arrested and taken away.

29. *Thomas Parry*, Elizabeth's treasurer, by Holbein. (Windsor Castle, Royal Library. © 1990 Her Majesty The Queen)

Sir Robert Tyrwhitt now set about interrogating Elizabeth. He had been sent by the Lord Protector, with instructions that he was to find enough evidence to convict Thomas and, if possible, incriminate Elizabeth at the same time. Gripped by a dreadful fear, she saw that if she made one mistake in her answers she could find herself in the Tower too. She was only fifteen, but her skill in dealing with Tyrwhitt impressed him. 'I assure Your Grace', he wrote to Somerset, 'she hath a very good wit and nothing is got from her but by great policy'. Her replies were bland, neutral and innocent. She even wrote

30. *Edward Seymour, Duke of Somerset*, Lord Protector of England, by M de Heere. (Muncaster Castle: photograph, Courtauld Institute of Art)

politely to the Lord Protector himself, pointing out some tiny, unimportant fact she had forgotten to mention before. Her version of events tallied exactly with the stories told by Parry and the Ashleys, so that Sir Robert was forced to report testily, 'They all sing one song!'

He was convinced that she knew more than she was telling. 'I do see it in her face that she is guilty', he wrote, but try as he might he could not persuade her to say anything about Thomas or her attendants and in the end he had to ride back to London empty-handed. Parry and the Ashleys were soon released, but for Thomas Seymour there could be no reprieve. The Lord Protector was convinced that his brother had been planning to murder him, and he refused to see him lest his own resolve weaken. Thomas went to the block on 20 March 1549. 'This day died a man with much wit and very little judgment', Elizabeth is supposed to have remarked. The words are almost certainly apocryphal, but they probably summed up her reaction. She was deeply affected by his death but she had long since learned that, in the dangerous world of Tudor politics, self-preservation mattered before all else.

That summer she was ill with nephritis, the kidney disease which was to plague her for several years, but as soon as she was able she resumed her studies. Her tutor, William Grindal, had died of the plague the previous year, and on her own insistence he had been replaced by Roger Ascham. She and Roger both had fierce tempers and after one violent argument with her he rode off to Cambridge and stayed there for several months.

They made up their quarrel eventually, and Roger was safely back by the summer of 1550, reading the classics with Elizabeth each day and boasting to his continental friends about her abilities. Sir Thomas More's daughters might be justly famous, he wrote, but 'my illustrious mistress the Lady Elizabeth shines like a star . . . So much solidity of understanding, such courtesy united with dignity, have never been observed at so early an age. She hath the most ardent love of the true religion and of the best kind of literature. The constitution of her mind is exempt from female weakness and she is endued with a masculine power of application. No apprehension can be quicker than hers, no memory more retentive . . .'

She was a formidable young lady, imperious, sharp-tongued and alarmingly accomplished. Like her mother she kept an eye on every item of expenditure and because Thomas Parry had been careless with her household accounts in the past, she insisted on scrutinising and signing every page of the account book. She did not have vast financial resources, so economising became a way of life with her. She made few major purchases. Mr Warren the tailor supplied her clothes, wine was brought from France and once she ordered a new walnut table, but for the most part her expenditure was modest: brooms to clean her chamber, a new Bible, or lute strings from John Baptist.

In the usual way, most of her provisions came from her own estates and the kitchens were kept well supplied with veal, bacon, mutton, boar, oxen and poultry as well as eggs, barley and wheat. The customary diet was supplemented by gifts from well-wishers: a cygnet, some sturgeon or a few partridges. A group of Cambridge scholars arrived one day with apples, and another time a woman brought a basket of peas. The local people knew her well, for she loved to be out of doors, walking, riding and hunting on her lands. She would pace impatiently along the gallery when really bad weather kept her in, and if she was not reading she would be sewing, playing the virginals or dancing.

Occasionally, she visited London. The Seymour scandal had faded into the

31. *Mary Tudor*, Elizabeth's sister, in 1544 when she was twenty-eight, by Master John. (National Portrait Gallery, London)

past, and she was graciously received by King Edward. Mary found it distasteful to stay at her fervently Protestant brother's palaces and so Elizabeth attracted particular attention when she came, all the more so because her chosen way of dressing made her stand out. Amongst the rich and colourful satins and silks of the ladies she appeared in sober black and white.

In part, her costume emphasised her chosen role as the decorous, Protestant sister of the King: in part it underlined her own royalty, for black and white had always been special colours with almost magical properties. She was tall and lithe, and if her dominating aquiline nose and her thin cheeks gave her a striking resemblance to her grandfather, King Henry VII, people did not see

32. *Edward VI and the Pope*, an anti-papal allegory by an unknown artist of 1548–9, showing Henry VIII on his deathbed, Edward enthroned, Somerset on his left and, at the table, from left to right, Northumberland, Cranmer and Bedford. The other councillors are unidentified.
(National Portrait Gallery, London)

it. Instead, looking at her red hair and her white skin, they nudged each other and said that she was the image of her father.

In the spring of 1552, Protestant Englishmen were particularly eager to point out the similarity, for everyone was preoccupied with fears for the future. Promising young Edward VI, their pious, intellectual King, had fallen seriously ill with pulmonary tuberculosis and they were faced with the dreadful prospect that if he died, Mary would succeed. What then would happen to the Reformed Church? Increasingly, they pinned their hopes to Elizabeth, looking to her for leadership in the coming crisis.

Lord Protector Somerset was dead by now, ousted and executed by his rival John Dudley, Earl of Warwick. Long a member of the Privy Council, Dudley was well known at court. His children often played with Edward and Elizabeth, his son Robert becoming one of her favourite companions. A determined adventurer, Warwick had finally managed to seize power, making himself Edward's chief minister and accumulating a clutch of titles and offices. Now Duke of Northumberland, he was carrying Somerset's Protestant policies still further and he knew that if Mary succeeded he would fall from power. Edward was equally worried by the thought of his half-sister inheriting his throne, and when in May 1553 his doctors warned him that he had only three months to live, he and Northumberland devised a plan. He would bequeath his crown to his cousin's daughter, Lady Jane Grey, who had recently married one of Northumberland's sons, Lord Guildford Dudley. Both Mary and Elizabeth would be excluded from the succession, on the grounds that they were illegitimate.

Edward's Privy Councillors, despite their Protestantism, did not like the idea. Henry VIII's will had been given the force of law by parliament. It could not be set aside. Nevertheless, when the King called them in separately and urged them to agree, they could not deny him his last wish and so in the end they all gave their consent. When he died on 7 July, Northumberland had Lady Jane Grey proclaimed Queen of England.

Jane did not want to be Queen. She had not wanted to marry Lord Guildford Dudley. She despised him and she hated his ambitious father. She would far rather have been left in peace with her books, but she had no choice. She had to put on jewel-encrusted clothes and go in procession to the state apartments of the Tower of London to await her coronation, while her father-in-law rode with his sons for East Anglia, to hunt down Mary Tudor.

Mary had fled to her estates there as soon as she had heard the news. She realised that she was in deadly danger, but she was convinced of the justice of her cause. She was the great King Henry's only legitimate child and so she was the rightful Queen. She issued a proclamation rallying her subjects and soon supporters were flocking to her, Roman Catholics and Protestants alike. Within a fortnight Northumberland's attempt to divert the succession from her collapsed. He surrendered and was taken back to London. 'May I go home now?' asked Lady Jane, but of course she could not. Instead of being a Queen preparing for her coronation, she had become a prisoner under threat of death, charged with high treason.

Elizabeth was at Hatfield throughout the crisis. When she first learned of Edward's serious illness she set out for London to visit him, but she was only halfway there when she received a message telling her to go back. It was Northumberland's doing, of course. He could not afford to have her at court, complicating his plans. As soon as she knew that Jane had been proclaimed Queen, Elizabeth took to her bed, saying that she was far too ill to travel anywhere. Once she heard that the rising was over, however, she got up and prepared to ride to the capital. If she did not show her loyalty to Mary, her enemies would accuse her of setting herself up as a rival Protestant claimant and, in the present atmosphere of suspicion and uncertainty, even the most unfounded rumour could do her damage.

Mary and the Roman Catholics were in a mood of almost incredulous exaltation. At last the world had come right again. Their Church would be restored, Catherine of Aragon's cause would be vindicated and the dreadful events of past years could be forgotten. For Protestants, the prospect was very different. What would happen to their recently established Church? What, indeed, would happen to them? The future looked bleak.

Riding proudly at the head of an impressive entourage, Elizabeth reached London to find that Mary had not yet arrived. The citizens turned out to shout their approval as she passed and she smiled and waved graciously to them. She had not been forgotten after all. She might have few friends at the new Queen's court, but the ordinary people were offering her their goodwill, and that could be useful.

At last, word came that Mary's procession was approaching, and Elizabeth went to the outskirts of the city to meet her. In an atmosphere charged with emotion, everyone watched as Anne Boleyn's child moved forward to demonstrate her loyalty to Catherine of Aragon's daughter. At nineteen, Elizabeth towered over the tiny figure of the Queen. Mary was thirty-seven, and she looked older, tired and worn after all the excitement of past weeks. Elizabeth knelt before her, Mary smiled, raised her up and embraced her. It seemed that they were to be friends. Other introductions followed, Elizabeth presenting her own retinue, and finally, when the procession moved off again, she was in the place of honour immediately behind the Queen.

33. *Lady Jane Grey* in about 1545, by Master John.
(National Portrait Gallery, London)

3

QUEEN MARY

IN SUBSEQUENT DAYS, Mary continued to give Elizabeth the position of heir presumptive to the throne, walking hand in hand with her on state occasions and presenting her with valuable gifts. There was always a feeling of tension, however, a simmering hostility between the two sisters. Mary admitted to the Imperial ambassador, Simon Renard, that, try as she might, she could not set aside her loathing for the Concubine's daughter. Whenever she looked at Elizabeth she was reminded of Anne Boleyn and everything that had gone before. For her part, Elizabeth viewed Mary with resentment and apprehension. She had a horror of being in anyone's power. She knew that she must submit to Mary because Mary was Queen of England, but she was afraid of what would follow.

While the Queen assembled her new Privy Council and set about restoring the old religion and her mother's reputation, Elizabeth made a public parade of her Protestantism. The rest of the court might go meekly along to Mass with Mary, but Elizabeth stayed away from the Chapel Royal. Her absence did not go unnoticed, of course, and Renard drew the worst possible conclusion, suspecting her of plotting to raise a new Protestant rebellion. He believed that

34. *Edward Courtenay, Earl of Devon*, by an unknown artist. (Woburn Abbey)

she was greatly to be feared. 'She is a spirit of incantation', he told one of his friends. Few seemed able to resist her spell.

She had already gathered around her a group of lively young courtiers who were finding Mary's circle dull beyond belief. With them came Edward Courtenay, a significant figure. Descended from the Plantagenet kings of England, he had had a strange upbringing. His father had been executed for treason and he had spent most of his life in the Tower of London with his mother. She had seen to it that he received an excellent education: there had been little else for him to do but study. He was pleasant and cultivated but completely unused to the ways of the world.

When Mary came to the throne, one of her first acts had been to free the Roman Catholic prisoners in the Tower. Courtenay's mother had been one of her closest friends. Now she became the Queen's constant companion, while Courtenay set out joyfully to sample all the pleasures so long denied him. Soon people were saying that he would make an ideal husband for Mary, or for Elizabeth.

Determined that her sister should convert, preferably before parliament met in October to restore the Roman Catholic Church, the Queen ordered Elizabeth to attend the Chapel Royal services. Elizabeth sent her messenger away with a very rude reply. Mary then dispatched Privy Councillors with dire warnings. People of consequence who displeased the monarch were liable to find themselves in the Tower. Elizabeth feared that most of all, and after six weeks of obduracy, she gave in. She requested an audience with the Queen.

They met privately, in a long gallery, with only a lady-in-waiting each for company. Elizabeth knelt, weeping, and assured Mary that she had meant no harm. She had been brought up as a Protestant, and she knew no other form of worship. If Mary would allow her to have books and a learned teacher, she would gladly take instruction. Temporarily reassured, the Queen smiled and agreed. Shortly afterwards, Elizabeth went to her first Mass, grumbling loudly for the benefit of the Protestant bystanders.

Her apparent conversion deceived nobody. Even the French ambassador, who had instructions to cultivate her, said openly that she was acting out of fear, not fervour, and Mary summoned her to a second audience to tax her with hypocrisy. There was no deceit, cried Elizabeth, she was genuinely trying to accept Roman Catholicism. She seemed sincere enough, thought Mary, noticing how she trembled from head to foot as she spoke. Perhaps Renard was wrong, but even if the girl were not plotting to lead the Protestants in rebellion she must still convert for the good of her immortal soul.

Elizabeth felt that she was being driven into a corner. She had thought at first that she was powerful enough to go her own way, but she saw now that her sister would never allow her to do as she chose, least of all where religion was concerned. Mary was determined to change her for her own good, as well as being set on redressing past wrongs. That autumn, one humiliation followed another for Elizabeth. Parliament passed an act ruling that Henry VIII's divorce from Catherine of Aragon had been illegal. In other words, Henry and Anne Boleyn had never been married at all, and their daughter was illegitimate. Further to emphasise the point, Mary sent her sister a gift of a little gold book to wear from her belt. When Elizabeth opened it, she found that it contained miniature portraits of Henry VIII and Catherine of Aragon.

People were even saying that Mary wanted to exclude her from the succession. There were other possible heirs. Henry VIII had had two sisters. Mary, the younger, had been the grandmother of Lady Jane Grey, still a prisoner in

35. *Sir Thomas Wyatt the younger,*
who conspired against Queen Mary,
by an unknown artist.
(National Portrait Gallery, London)

the Tower. Margaret, the elder, was the mother of the Countess of Lennox. A lively, attractive woman with brown hair, a longish face and small, clever eyes, the Countess had been brought up at the English court like a royal princess. Moreover, she was a Roman Catholic. She and her husband, a Stewart with a strong claim to the throne of Scotland, divided their time between London and their Yorkshire estates. Now Mary began to give Lady Lennox precedence over Elizabeth at various court functions.

She did not, however, intend her cousin to succeed her. Mary had always meant to remain a virgin, but now that she had inherited the throne she realised, with a sinking heart, that it was her duty to marry and have children. Her people were anxious for her to take an English husband, but she had other plans. Her cousin Charles V was offering her his own son, Philip, and after hours of prayer and soul-searching she decided to accept him. Her subjects were horrified. Philip was a foreigner. He would interfere with domestic policies and drag England into expensive foreign wars, for Spain and France were continually fighting each other. Her ministers remonstrated and parliament protested against the match, but in vain. Mary had made up her mind, and she was not going to change it.

Elizabeth, staying at the royal manor of Ashridge, which was now hers, was approached by a Kentish gentleman named Sir Thomas Wyatt. She always denied afterwards that he had been in touch with her, but it seems certain that he did inform her of his plans. He intended to raise an armed rebellion and depose Mary, so that Elizabeth and Edward Courtenay could marry and rule England together. There is no evidence that Elizabeth encouraged Wyatt or even sent him an answer, but she did begin gathering armed men around her, for her protection, so she said.

Before long, the plot began to go badly wrong. Wyatt had expected Courtenay to join gladly in his conspiracy, but the young man had other ideas. He wanted to marry Mary, not Elizabeth, and after a great deal of tiresome procrastination, he confessed everything. When Wyatt discovered that his secret was out, he decided to go ahead at once, even though his preparations were not complete. He had nothing to lose. He would march on London right away, and so he sent a message to Elizabeth urging her to move further away from the capital, to a place of greater safety.

Before she could either comply with his advice or go to London to vindicate herself before the Queen, Elizabeth was taken seriously ill with a high fever and swelling of her limbs, presumably a recurrence of the nephritis. She could not go anywhere, even when a peremptory message arrived from Mary summoning her to court. All she could do was to toss and turn on her sickbed and wait for reports of what was happening further south. Wyatt was marching on London, she heard, albeit with a far smaller force than he had hoped to raise. The Londoners were in a panic. The Lord Chancellor was urging Mary to flee to Windsor, but she was refusing. Instead, she put on her crown, went to the Guildhall and rallied her subjects with a rousing speech. Finally, word came that the rebellion had been crushed. Wyatt and Courtenay were in prison, and the Queen was going to execute Lady Jane Grey, her husband and her father before they caused trouble too. Once again, she summoned Elizabeth to court.

A few days later, two of the royal doctors arrived at Ashridge. Their principal intention was to see if Elizabeth really was ill, but Mary had sent Elizabeth's great-uncle Lord William Howard with them, possibly in a gesture of reassurance. They found her pale, weak and still suffering from the swelling in her body and limbs. She was past the worst, though, and they were sure that she would soon be able to travel to court to affirm her loyalty. On 12 February 1554, the very day that Lady Jane Grey was executed, Elizabeth left Ashridge. She knew very well that Mary was going to accuse her of complicity in Wyatt's plot, and she was terrified of what would happen when she reached London. Weakness and apprehension brought her to the point of collapse, and several times it seemed that she would faint as she was helped out into the litter the Queen had sent for her.

The journey was very slow, for the doctors insisted that their patient should take it in easy stages. They travelled no more than six miles a day, but when they arrived on the outskirts of the city Elizabeth gave orders for the curtains of the litter to be drawn back, so that everyone could see her. She was determined to enlist the sympathy of the Londoners. She was all in white and, according to Simon Renard, 'her countenance was pale, her look proud,

36. *William Paulet, 1st Marquess of Winchester,* holding his Treasurer's white wand of office, painted by an unknown artist.
(National Portrait Gallery, London)

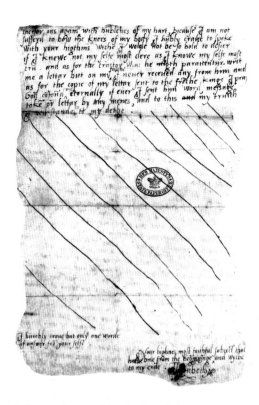

37. Letter from Elizabeth to Queen Mary, begging for an audience before being sent to the Tower.

(Public Record Office, London)

lofty and superbly disdainful, an expression which she assumed to disguise the mortification she felt'.

When she finally arrived at Whitehall, she was told that she had been allocated rooms as far away from the rest of the court as possible. She was also told that Mary did not want to see her. Renard had spent long hours convincing the Queen of Elizabeth's guilt. Confined to her apartments, she waited in trepidation. On 15 March, Wyatt was condemned to death. On the 17th, two ominous visitors arrived at her lodgings. The Marquess of Winchester and the Earl of Sussex had come, they said, to escort her to the Tower of London.

Panic-stricken, she could think only of death and Thomas Seymour's end. He had been sent to the Tower for execution. So had her own mother, her stepmother Katherine Howard and now Lady Jane Grey. Was she herself going to be next? Desperately she asked for pen, ink and paper so that she could beg Mary for an audience, assure her of her innocence, plead for her freedom. 'I never practised, counselled nor consented to anything that might be prejudicial to your person in any way or dangerous to the state by any means', she wrote, and she recalled how Lord Protector Somerset always used to say that if only he had agreed to see his brother Thomas before his execution, that death sentence would never have been carried out. If Mary would agree to see Elizabeth, all misunderstandings would be removed.

When she had said all she could, Elizabeth took her pen and drew long, diagonal lines across the rest of the page. No one was gong to forge any extra words at the end of what she had written. Finally, she signed herself, 'Your Highness's most faithful subject, that hath been from the beginning and will be to my end, Elizabeth', and then she threw down the pen. Sussex and Winchester were fuming. They had orders to take her to the Tower by barge, for Mary did not want her attracting sympathy by riding through the streets.

She had delayed for so long that they had missed the tide. They would not be able to sail again until midnight, and if they went in the dark there was the danger that she might somehow escape. Reluctantly, they decided to wait until the following morning and, telling her so, they went away.

It was a respite, but a very brief one. She waited anxiously, but no message arrived from the Queen. Morning came, and there was still no word. Sussex and Winchester reappeared with the information that Mary would not see her. Indeed, the Queen had been furious with them and she had told them in no uncertain terms that they should never have allowed Elizabeth to write the letter. They would never have dared do such a thing if her father had been alive, she had declared bitterly. 'The Lord's will be done. I am contented', said Elizabeth, and she allowed them to escort her through the gardens of Whitehall Palace to the landing stage where the barge was waiting.

It was Palm Sunday, and it was raining heavily. This time the tide was right, and all too soon they were mooring at the Water Gate of the Tower, known in more recent times as Traitors' Gate. Winchester and Sussex stepped from the barge and began to mount the stairs to the landing stage. Elizabeth refused to move. Winchester turned back and ordered her curtly to get out. She had no choice in the matter, he said. He offered her his cloak, against the rain, but she dashed it angrily aside, saying in a loud voice as she climbed the steps, 'Here landeth as true a subject, being prisoner, as ever landed at these stairs and before thee, O God, I speak it, having none other friend but Thee!'

When she reached the top, she sat down suddenly on the wet stones and would not get up again. 'Madam', said the Lieutenant of the Tower, coming anxiously over to her, 'you had best come out of the rain, for you sit unwholesomely.' 'Better sit here than in a worse place', she retorted, 'for God knoweth, not I, whither you will bring me!' Her gentleman usher was standing nearby, and when he heard her say that he burst into tears. She rounded on him in an instant, rebuking him sharply for giving way to his feelings. His duty was to comfort her, not to dismay her, she snapped. However, she got up and went with them to the Bell Tower, where she was given a large room on the second floor. Winchester was all for locking her in, but Sussex quickly reminded him that, whatever her circumstances now, she was still the heir to the throne. If Mary were to die, they could find themselves answering to this young woman for the way they had treated her. The door was left unlocked.

Her own servants were allowed to prepare her food, to make sure that it was not poisoned, and she was permitted to see her doctor, but when she asked for pens and paper she was told curtly that she could not have them. She was not to write to the Queen again, nor must she try to pass messages to other prisoners in the Tower: her childhood friend Lord Robert Dudley, for example, who had been there since his arrest for his part in his father's conspiracy to put Lady Jane Grey on the throne.

Used to an active life, Elizabeth longed for exercise and the open air. At first when she asked, she was told that she could walk up and down in the Queen's apartments. This was no pleasure, for they were dark and gloomy: the shutters were kept firmly closed to prevent her from seeing anyone outside. She complained bitterly, and after some days they said she could go out onto the walls of the Tower for a short distance, under the scrutiny of her warders.

That was hardly satisfactory, but the Constable eventually relented and gave her the use of a little enclosed garden. No one else was supposed to go there, but the four-year-old son of one of the Tower officials found his way in one day and he became a friend, holding long conversations with her, bringing her a bunch of flowers. Her guards at first thought that the child's visits were harmless but someone suggested that that he might be used to carry messages between Elizabeth and the other prisoners and he was told he must never go into the garden again.

Wyatt was beheaded on 11 April 1554, but the Privy Council were deeply divided about what to do with Elizabeth. Some, like Lord Chancellor Gardiner, thought that the only way to remove her from the succession was to execute her, but the lawyers were unable to provide any real evidence against her, and so she had to stay where she was, in an agony of suspense.

On 4 May she was thrown into a panic when she saw a large detachment of soldiers march up to the Tower. She was sure that they had come for her execution, and she asked desperately if Lady Jane Grey's scaffold had been taken down yet. It had been removed, she was told, and the reason the soldiers were there was that Sir Henry Bedingfield was taking over from Sir John Gage as Constable. Was he the sort of man who would commit a secret murder if ordered to do so, she asked nervously. Certainly not, they replied. He was a high-principled former ambassador who would never dream of doing such a thing. For the moment she was reassured, but a fortnight later all her terrors returned when she was told to prepare for a journey.

She had no idea where she was going. She was taken outside, to find Sir Henry Bedingfield and Lord Williams of Thame waiting with a litter for her and an escort of a hundred horsemen. She climbed into the litter, convinced that her last hour had come, and her procession moved off in the direction of Richmond. She could only think that the Queen was sending her to a more remote place so that they could do away with her without anyone knowing. 'This night I think to die', she said despairingly to Lord Williams, but he smiled at her and told her that she need have no such fears. She was safe with him.

By the time they reached Windsor on the following day, people had heard that she was coming, and they were lining the roadside, handing food and flowers into her litter, shouting kind messages. Surely this would not be allowed if some dreadful fate awaited her. They spent a night at Williams's

38. Sir Henry Bedingfield, Elizabeth's gaoler, by an unknown artist. (The National Trust, at Oxburgh Hall)

39. The Tower of London, from
the south-east.
(Photograph, A F Kersting)

40. Traitors' Gate, where
Elizabeth arrived at the Tower
of London.
(Photograph, A F Kersting)

own house at Thame, and she began to feel much better. Perhaps he told her then that her destination was the royal palace of Woodstock in Oxfordshire, where she would remain under Bedingfield's supervision.

The building was dilapidated, but rooms in the gatehouse had been prepared for her with some of her own and some of the Queen's furnishings. There was hardly any space for her servants, but they were able to find lodgings in the village. Thomas Parry installed himself in the local inn and, much to Sir Henry's annoyance, began to receive a stream of visitors full of court news and all the latest gossip.

Elizabeth's health was not good that summer. Her face and arms swelled up again with 'waterish humours', said the royal doctors who were sent to examine her. After their treatment she began to feel better and she embarked on a lively running battle with her gaoler. Sir Henry took his responsibilities very seriously. He referred every decision, great and small, to the Privy Council. Elizabeth found that irritating, but she was not afraid of him and she amused herself by treating him to rages, stony silences, imperious orders and malicious laughter – the very kind of behaviour Anne Boleyn had used to annoy her adversaries.

She complained about the women sent to wait on her, demanded an English bible, swore that she had been promised access to the parkland round about and managed to smuggle in books to read. She also insisted that he write to the Queen on her behalf, but that did no good, for Mary was still refusing to accept any messages from her. This impasse might have lasted indefinitely, but on 19 July Prince Philip sailed into Southampton aboard *The Holy Ghost* and Elizabeth gained a powerful if unlikely ally.

He had come for his wedding to Mary. A long-chinned, dapper young

42. Woodstock Palace, an early eighteenth-century view.
(Royal Commission on the Historical Monuments of England)

widower, half-Hapsburg, half-Portuguese, he had been forced into this match by his father. Charles V was determined to keep England as his ally and this seemed the simplest way of doing it. There were complications, of course. It was unlikely that Mary, at her age, would have a child and if she did become pregnant she would most probably die in childbirth. Philip was therefore under orders to have a care for the future. He was to make sure that if anything happened to his wife, either he himself or Elizabeth should succeed to the throne immediately. Henry II of France must at all costs be prevented from inserting his own candidate.

With these instructions in mind, Philip obediently went to his wedding in Winchester Cathedral. He was depressed to discover that his bride was middle-aged, plain and unappealing. To make matters worse, she fell passionately in love with him. He had difficulty in concealing his distaste for her, but his father's ambassador was constantly at his elbow, reminding him of his duty. Trying his best to implement his orders, he suggested to Mary that she should bring her sister back to court. Her response was chilly. She would do almost anything for him, but not that. Elizabeth remained at Woodstock.

The months passed not unpleasantly for her there and, well aware of the political situation, she wrote to Philip asking for his protection. He was now trying to persuade Mary that if only they could find a suitable husband for her sister, all their worries would be at an end. His own eight-year-old son Don Carlos was one possibility, he thought, or perhaps Charles V's favourite general, the Duke of Savoy. Kept in check by a sensible, Roman Catholic husband, Elizabeth would surely settle down. Better still, she would have to leave England and live abroad with her husband.

Before anything could be arranged, everyone's attention was diverted by a new development. Mary announced that she was pregnant. She seemed to have all the appropriate symptoms, but Philip and many of the courtiers were doubtful. She was so old and unhealthy it hardly seemed possible. He took the opportunity, however, of raising yet again the question of Elizabeth. At this important time she ought to be at court where he could keep an eye on her. Should anything, heaven forbid, happen to the Queen, her half-sister might raise a rebellion and then his own life would be in danger. Mary was at once all solicitude. Of course nothing must threaten her beloved consort. He was right. She would bring the girl back.

In April 1555, Sir Henry Bedingfield was instructed to escort his prisoner to Hampton Court. Both were equally delighted. When they arrived, no official party was waiting to greet them. Instead, Elizabeth was hustled in through a back door and given apartments near Philip's. For the first few days she was allowed to see no one, but gradually she was permitted to have visitors. Some of the Privy Councillors came, and one evening a lady of the Queen's household brought her a rich dress with instructions to put it on at once. Philip was coming to see her.

No description of their meeting has survived, but the encounter must have gone well for a few weeks later Mary announced that she would grant her sister an audience. A lady-in-waiting came for Elizabeth late at night and took her across the gardens to the part of the palace where the Queen was staying. Admitted to Mary's presence at last, Elizabeth threw herself on her knees and vowed that she was innocent of any part in Wyatt's conspiracy. According to one account, Philip was concealed throughout the interview behind the tapestry, listening intently to everything that was said. When Elizabeth finished speaking, Mary sighed and muttered in Spanish, 'Who knows?' As ever, she was unable to gauge the truth of what her sister was saying.

The Queen believed that her child would be born in June. Reclining on cushions on the floor, she waited with increasing despair throughout that summer, but no child was born. Mary was probably suffering from an ovarian tumour, with consequent swelling of the body and the cessation of periods. By the beginning of August she had to admit that there was no baby. Unable to stand her company any longer, Philip left for Brussels, promising to return quickly. A few weeks later, Elizabeth was allowed to go to Hatfield. Delighted to be free at last, she resumed her previous way of life as an important royal lady, running her estates, studying her favourite classics, hunting and listening to music.

Philip stayed away for many months. His father had decided to abdicate, making him ruler of the Netherlands and King of Spain. The title of Holy Roman Emperor went to Charles's own brother Ferdinand, for Charles had always felt that his inheritance was far too large for any one man. Almost all Philip's interests were on the continent now, but he continued to protect Elizabeth. On several occasions Mrs Ashley and other members of her household were arrested for seditious activities but she herself was never held.

She did not feel safe, however, for she knew that Mary and Philip were still determined to marry her to a foreign husband. There were frightening rumours that Mary planned to have her kidnapped and carried off to Spain, so that she could be forced into marriage with Don Carlos. Perhaps these were merely wild stories, but in the autumn of 1556 there was a much more serious threat. The details of what happened are not altogether clear, but it seems that Mary summoned her to court and tried to compel her to marry the Duke of Savoy, threatening her with the Tower or even with death if she did not obey.

For all her defiance, Elizabeth was afraid of her sister. She knew how implacable Mary could be and she knew her fierce Tudor temper. Frightened though she was, however, she could never agree to take a foreign husband

43. Hampton Court Palace, the Clock Court.
(Photograph, A F Kersting)

44. The Tudor Kitchen at Hampton Court Palace.
(Photograph, A F Kersting)

and leave the country. She refused point blank. Afterwards, she sent in a panic to ask the French ambassador if she could flee to France. The ambassador replied tersely that if she hoped to inherit the throne of England she must stay where she was. Elizabeth stayed. She did not remain in London, however. She left after a mere week, returning to the security of Hatfield. Once there, she fell ill with jaundice.

Mary took no further action. She was desperate not to annoy Philip, for she longed for his return, and she knew that he would disapprove if she took any action against Elizabeth. He had said he would be away for no more than a few weeks. The weeks had become months, and in the end he did not arrive back until March 1557. Mary was overjoyed, but his stay was to be pitifully short. He had not come to be with her, but to conduct some important business. He was at war with France, and he wanted England to join him.

45. *Queen Mary I* by Hans Eworth, 1554.
(National Portrait Gallery, London)

46. *Bishop Bonner burning a man's hand with a torch*, woodcut by an unknown artist.
(National Portrait Gallery, London)

As soon as agreement had been given, he went back to the continent.

Mary was becoming more and more unpopular with her subjects. Ignoring the advice of Philip and her Privy Councillors, she had begun persecuting the Protestants and nearly three hundred men and women had been burned at the stake, including Elizabeth's godfather, Archbishop Cranmer. The war was going badly and Calais, England's stronghold since the Middle Ages, was captured by the French. It was a dreadful disgrace, and Mary was heartbroken.

At best, her subjects felt a contemptuous pity for her and, as her power waned, Elizabeth's influence grew. She might not be accepted by Mary as her successor, but everyone else knew that Henry VIII's will still stood and more and more people were coming to Hatfield to pledge their support to her. The King of Sweden even sent envoys to propose that she should marry his heir, Prince Eric. She replied politely that she could not enter into any negotiation and he must approach Mary about it first.

The sisters saw each other for the last time in January 1558. Philip's ambassador, the Count de Feria, urged Mary to bring Elizabeth to court again and, still hoping in vain to please her husband, she agreed. Ill and depressed, the Queen felt all her old fears and suspicions rise to the surface once more and she told people that Elizabeth was no sister of hers. Henry VIII was not the girl's father. Anne Boleyn had been a whore, and Elizabeth was the child of one of Anne's lovers.

Distressing though it was, none of that really mattered now, for Mary was obviously nearing the end of her life. After another false pregnancy, she realised it herself, and in November she sent word to Elizabeth that she would allow her to succeed to the throne providing she maintained the Roman Catholic faith as it was and paid all Mary's debts. Elizabeth agreed.

A day or two later, the Queen lapsed into unconsciousness. The Count de Feria arrived back in England and on 9 November he presided over a meeting of the Privy Council which confirmed Elizabeth's rights. He then rode to Brockett Hall, a mansion near Hatfield, where she was staying. He found her in a mood of cheerful excitement. She knew that it could not be long now. For days people had been flocking to her with assurances of loyalty. She dined that night with the Count and her friend Lady Clinton. 'We laughed and enjoyed ourselves a great deal', Feria told Philip. She assured him in private afterwards that she was grateful for Philip's past help, and said that she would maintain the friendship between them, but the Count was uneasy. 'She is a

47. *Prince Eric of Sweden*, painted in later life as King Eric XIV,
probably by Steven van der Meulen.
(Gripsholm, Sweden: photograph, Svenska museiforeningen 1990)

very vain and clever woman', he reported, and he feared she might favour
neither Spain nor France but go her own way.

Elizabeth went back to Hatfield after that, to wait. Mary lay at St James's,
still unconscious. On 16 November, the Lord Chancellor and the Privy Council
went into her chamber for the reading of her will. The following morning,
she seemed to respond slightly when Mass was said at her bedside, but
between 10 and 11 o'clock she died. Parliament was dissolved, the ports were
closed and the Privy Councillors rode for Hatfield. According to tradition,
they found Elizabeth sitting in the park beneath an oak tree, reading her
Greek bible. They told her the news and she put down her book and knelt.
'This is the Lord's doing, and it is marvellous in our eyes', she said. At the
age of twenty-five, she was Queen of England.

4

QUEEN ELIZABETH

NOW THAT the moment had come, Elizabeth knew exactly what to do. That very same day she made her first appointment, and it was a vital one. William Cecil would be her principal Secretary of State. She had known him since the days when she stayed with Katherine Parr and he was one of the able young Protestants who had come to the house to discuss classics, religion and the latest court gossip. Now he was thirty-eight and in the years between he had gained considerable experience of government. He had managed to serve both Lord Protector Somerset and the Duke of Northumberland as Secretary of State, and he had even survived under Queen Mary, albeit in a minor position.

In recent months he had been lying low, to avoid religious controversy, but he and Elizabeth had kept in touch, for he was the surveyor of her estates.

48. *William Cecil*, Elizabeth's Secretary of State, painted in the 1560s
by or after Arnold van Brounckhorst.
(National Portrait Gallery, London)

49. The Great Hall at the Old Palace of Hatfield, where Elizabeth held her first Privy Council.
(Photograph, A F Kersting)

50. *Lady Catherine Grey*, Jane's sister, and a possible claimant of Elizabeth's throne, in a miniature possibly by L Teerlinc.
(By courtesy of the Board of Trustees of the Victoria and Albert Museum)

She knew that she needed his foresight, his devotion to the crown and his capacity for meticulous hard work. He would look after all her correspondence, not merely reading the letters that came in but drafting her replies, and he was also to be responsible for foreign policy and the secret service.

On the following day, Elizabeth met her new Privy Council for the first

49

51. *Sir Nicholas Bacon*, Elizabeth's Lord Keeper of the Great Seal and brother-in-law of Cecil, painted in the year of his death by an unknown artist.
(National Portrait Gallery, London)

52. *William Parr, Marquess of Northampton*, brother of Katherine Parr and one of Elizabeth's new Privy Councillors, by Holbein.
(Windsor Castle, Royal Library. © 1990 Her Majesty The Queen)

time. She had not dismissed all those who had served her sister. That would have been foolish. She needed men of experience, and a certain continuity. She therefore reappointed thirteen of Mary's councillors and added nine of her own, led by Cecil, his brother-in-law Sir Nicholas Bacon and Katherine Parr's brother, the Marquess of Northampton. Cecil was the youngest of them. Almost all the rest were over fifty.

The council formed, she lost no time in announcing other appointments to the government and to her household. Naturally enough, old friends were rewarded for past loyalty. Thomas Parry, her faithful cofferer, was made Treasurer of the Royal Household. Kate Ashley would be Mistress of the Maids of Honour while her husband took up the position of Keeper of the Jewel House. Roger Ascham was invited to become Latin secretary.

Her great-uncle, Lord William Howard, who had so successfully safe-guarded her interests at the time of the Wyatt conspiracy, was already Lord Chamberlain and he would continue in that office. Lord Williams of Thame, who had been so kind to her on the way to Woodstock, became President of the Welsh Marches. Her childhood playmate, Lord Robert Dudley, would be Master of the Horse, Lady Clinton's husband became Lord Admiral, her cousin Harry Carey took command of her personal guard and his sister Catherine entered the household as one of her gentlewomen. Elizabeth had dismissed every one of Mary's ladies. She would never have been able to trust them. Instead, she chose her own friends and relatives, including two who were rival claimants for her throne. Margaret, Countess of Lennox and Lady Jane Grey's sister Catherine would be best kept close by her, where she could see what they were doing.

The arrangements made, Elizabeth set off for London on 23 November. More than a thousand men and women rode with her. Just outside the city walls the Lord Mayor was waiting with an official deputation to welcome her. He made an address and then presented his various companions. She smiled graciously and allowed them to kiss her hand, but when she saw the stout figure of Bishop Bonner of London bustling forward she snatched her hand away from this well-known persecutor of Protestants.

She spent the next few days at Lord North's house, conducting business, seeing a constant stream of visitors, holding Privy Council meetings and then on the afternoon of 28 November she rode to the Tower. The last time she had approached that grim fortress it had been as a captive, in terror of her life. Now, clad in purple velvet, she rode up, to the sound of trumpets and a half-hour-long salute from the guns. Even so, the memory of that former occasion was vividly with her and she stopped to gaze up at the walls of her former prison. 'Some have fallen from being Princes of this land to be prisoners in this place', she said at last. 'I am raised from being a prisoner in this place to be a Prince of this land. That dejection was a work of God's justice. This advancement is a work of His mercy.' With that, she went in to the state apartments.

Sir Henry Bedingfield was still Lieutenant of the Tower. She called him over, thanked him for his services to the crown and told him that he would be replaced. 'God forgive you the past, as I do', she said, and she added with a wry smile, 'Whenever I have one who requires to be safely and straitly kept, I will send him to you!'

One of her first duties was to arrange her sister's funeral, and whatever her personal feelings, the fact that Mary had been Queen of England meant that Elizabeth was determined that the service should be conducted with appropriate pomp. Since her death, Mary's body had lain at St James's Palace in the room next to her bedchamber. On 13 December the corpse was carried in procession to Westminster Abbey, a lifelike effigy in royal crown and robes

53. *Edward Fiennes, Lord Clinton,* Elizabeth's Lord Admiral, by Holbein. (Windsor Castle, Royal Library. © Her Majesty The Queen)

lying on the coffin. The following day, she was buried in Henry VII's chapel after a sermon by the Bishop of Winchester. He was a Roman Catholic, of course, and he took as his text, 'I praise the dead more than the living'. He told his congregation that they would have to obey Elizabeth since 'a living dog is better than a dead lion'. She did not attend the service herself, but she was furious when she heard and she kept him under house arrest for the next month.

Every moment of her time was occupied: there were so many people to see and there was so much business to be done. Monarchs were not expected to attend every Privy Council meeting, but Elizabeth was going regularly, determined to keep a close eye on all that was happening. She also pounced eagerly on incoming correspondence. One day William Cecil was highly indignant when he discovered that a foreign ambassador's letter had been taken straight to the Queen instead of being given to him first. To make matters worse, Elizabeth had actually discussed its contents with the messenger. That was a grave solecism. He rebuked the unfortunate man for approaching her at all, 'a matter of such weight being too much for a woman's knowledge'.

Cecil placed no reliance on female judgment. Past experience with Queen Mary had convinced him that women were unpredictable and over-emotional. He would far rather have worked for a man, and most of the other middle-aged gentlemen who served the new Queen would have agreed with him. They found Elizabeth baffling, as did the foreign ambassadors. She was 'a young lass who, although sharp, is without prudence' the Count de Feria told Philip II, but he had to admit that she 'seems to me incomparably more feared than her sister, and gives her orders and has her way as absolutely as her father did'. Moreover, she had a disturbing habit of coming out with some biting remark when he was least expecting it, or of saying something 'with great laughter, as if she could read the Count's secret thoughts'. It was all most disconcerting, and he could only conclude, 'She is a very strange sort of woman'.

Elizabeth was enjoying herself. After all the years of danger and isolation, she was suddenly at the centre of events, wielding supreme power, flattered, fawned upon, sought out by all who wished for favours. By now, she had established a regular routine. She liked to rise early and unless the weather was atrocious she set off at once for a brisk walk through her gardens, along the formal avenues, past the topiary hedges, the neat flower-beds and the statues. When she came in, she took breakfast in her Privy Chamber and then her secretaries arrived to kneel before her with the letters of the day and piles of documents for her signature.

If the Privy Council was meeting, she might go along to the council chamber. There she would sit listening intently to he advisers' views and then, when they had all spoken, she would give her own opinion, succinctly and with emphasis. Mary had been heard to complain once that she had spent a whole morning shouting at her council, to no purpose. Elizabeth had a different method and she was already establishing her authority over these weighty, sceptical men. She was always autocratic, brooking no familiarity or impertinence and she was unpredictable. No one ever knew what she would say or do next, not even Cecil, for she was forever changing her mind. Conscious that every one of these ambitious statesmen would have liked to control her, she deliberately cultivated her natural imperiousness, her changeability and her penchant for uttering disconcerting remarks.

Taken off guard for a moment, even these sophisticated courtiers were liable

54. *Sir Thomas Gresham,* Elizabeth's leading financial adviser and founder of the Royal Exchange, by an unknown Flemish artist, about 1565.
(National Portrait Gallery, London)

to give away more than they had intended, and apart from anything else their discomfiture amused her. She had a quick mind and she was easily bored. She had to do something to relieve the long hours of tedium during their debates. Sometimes the discussions in council were acrimonious, and then she would shout as loudly as Mary had ever done. Her quick temper was notorious, and when she emerged from a meeting in a rage she would retire to a quiet corner of her Privy Chamber and read until she had calmed down.

On mornings when there was not a meeting she would go on working on her state papers but she always liked to set aside some time for dancing. Half a dozen energetic galliards in the Presence Chamber always cheered her up. Dinner, the main meal of the day, was served at about noon, in the Privy Chamber. Elizabeth ate sparingly and she invariably watered down her wine. In the afternoon there might be more visitors to see. Foreign ambassadors were formally received in the Presence Chamber, with government officials and courtiers present. The Queen remained standing throughout these interviews, however long, and she conversed animatedly in Latin with the visiting envoys, impressing them with her fluency.

Sometimes there was a state banquet in the evening, but more often she permitted herself some recreation. She was devoted to music, both church and secular, and as well as listening to others perform, she herself played the lute and the virginal. After a light supper she loved a game of cards with some of the courtiers, but before the evening was over she returned to her papers again. Messengers were liable to arrive with dispatches at any time and Cecil and his colleagues were resigned to being called out at all hours to confer with the Queen. Many of her decisions were taken after midnight and reversed when morning came.

Her own personal attendants were on duty day and night. Early or late, she had some of her women with her: the four Ladies of the Bedchamber, the seven Ladies of the Privy Chamber or the two or three Ladies of the Presence Chamber, not to mention Mr and Mrs Ashley, her grooms, her gentleman usher, her dwarfs and her fool. She told her ladies at the very start that she did not want them discussing politics with her: that was not their role. However, there is no doubt that they did bring her news of what was happening at court and they were generally regarded as being intermediaries who could put someone's case quietly to Her Majesty when she was not taken up with other things.

Just before her first Christmas as Queen, she moved to Whitehall, her principal residence and the largest palace in Europe. Its scattered buildings covered more than twenty-three acres and its Privy Chamber was her pride and joy, for on the wall was Holbein's huge painting of Henry VIII and the Tudor dynasty. On Christmas morning the Bishop of Carlisle said Mass in her chapel. As soon as he began to elevate the Host for adoration, the Queen's voice rang out, telling him to lower the vessel at once. Protestants did not believe that the bread and wine became the body and blood of Christ and so they objected to this part of the service. There was a stunned silence. Glaring, the Bishop held it higher. The Queen was on her feet in an instant, marching out of the chapel in a fury. That same week she issued a proclamation ordering the Litany, the Lord's Prayer and other central parts of the service to be read out in English instead of Latin.

The scene in the Chapel Royal had embarrassing repercussions. Busy with the preparations for her coronation, she was unable to find any bishop who was willing to place the crown upon her head. The Archbishop of Canterbury should have officiated, but he had died within hours of Mary herself. Now Archbishop Heath of York told her tersely that as she had refused to witness the elevation of the Host she must be a heretic, and he could not crown her. One by one the other bishops also refused, until in the end Owen Oglethorpe, the Bishop of Carlisle, succumbed to royal pressure and agreed.

The royal tailors were hard at work altering small Mary's coronation robes to fit tall Elizabeth. Carpenters were building triumphal arches over the city streets and house owners were decorating the outsides of their dwellings with tapestries and banners. Hundreds of men were clearing and gravelling the highways. With the advice of her favourite astrologer, Dr John Dee, Elizabeth had chosen 15 January 1559 for her coronation and, on the previous Thursday, she went by barge to the Tower to spend the obligatory night or two before the ceremony.

On Saturday she emerged again, in a litter of gold brocade, drawn by two mules. Her personal bodyguard marched alongside, her scarlet-clad trumpeters announced her approach and Lord Robert Dudley, as Master of the

55. *Nicholas Heath, Archbishop of York* by Hans Eworth, 1566.
(National Portrait Gallery, London)

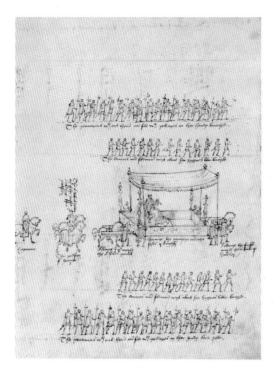

56. Drawing of Elizabeth's coronation procession, showing her beneath her fringed canopy, Lord Robert Dudley riding immediately behind. (The British Library)

Horse, was immediately behind her on a magnificent charger. Behind them rode all the lords and ladies in their crimson velvet and their dazzling jewels. The Queen herself was in a heavy royal robe of cloth of gold. Her hair was covered by a gold cap, and she wore a princess's gold crown set with precious gems.

Slowly, her procession made its state entry into the capital, stopping every few hundred yards so that she could admire the elaborate decorations, view carefully rehearsed pageants and hear welcoming Latin speeches. Elizabeth was in her element. She loved the compliments, the adulation, the reassuring flattery. When the crowds cheered, she waved in acknowledgment 'with a merry countenance' and when people surged forward to give her flowers, she stopped her litter and accepted them graciously. At each triumphal arch she delighted the performers by listening attentively to speeches from children dressed as cherubs, maidens in classical garb and an old man disguised as Father Time.

Great efforts had been made to please her. A three-tier representation of the Tudor dynasty included the figure of Queen Anne Boleyn, complete with crown and sceptre, Henry VIII by her side. Other pageants concentrated on the future, showing the defeat of Roman Catholicism and the triumph of Protestantism. In one, a sullen group of actors bore labels identifying them as 'Superstition', 'Hypocrisy', 'Ignorance' and 'Idolatry' while their cheerful, attractive counterparts at the other side declared themselves to be 'Pure Religion', 'Wisdom', 'Justice' and 'Fear of God'. Poems were presented to Elizabeth, praising her as Deborah, the chaste maiden who would restore Truth in the place of Error, and Father Time's daughter came down on a silken cord to give her an English bible. She kissed it, pressed it to her bosom, and promised to read it often.

At last she arrived at Westminster, where she would spend the night. Next morning, she went to the abbey to the pealing of all the bells in London. So many people pressed forward to see her that they nearly knocked over Lady Lennox, who was carrying her train. Inside the abbey, the walls had been hung with magnificent tapestries commissioned by Henry VIII from designs by Raphael. Following ancient tradition, she was led up to a lofty platform between the high altar and the choir, taken to the four corners and shown to the people. When they were asked if they wished her to be crowned Queen, they all shouted 'Yes', in noisy acclamation. What with 'the organs, fifes, trumpets and drums playing, and the bells also ringing it seemed as if the world were to come to an end', said an Italian who was in the congregation that day.

Descending from the platform, Elizabeth took her seat near the altar and the lengthy coronation ceremony began. Bishop Oglethorpe preached his sermon, administered the coronation oath, anointed her and crowned her. The lords all came to pay their homage, and after that there was a Latin Mass. For the most part, the ritual was just as it had been for Mary, for Henry VIII and for all Elizabeth's other royal predecessors, but there were innovations, introduced by the Queen's special command. When the Bishop administered the coronation oath, he read from an English bible which was held before him by William Cecil.

Other parts of the service were in English as well as in Latin, and although the Host was elevated during the Mass, Elizabeth did not witness it. She withdrew into a special pew concealed by a curtain. Again, when the time came for her subjects to take their oaths of homage, the bishops should have come first. She refused to allow that, and they had to wait until all the peers had knelt to her and vowed their allegiance.

It was nearly three o'clock in the afternoon when the Queen in her cloth of gold robe, her orb and sceptre in her hands, led the way to Westminster Hall for the coronation banquet. She was in her element, smiling, nodding and greeting everyone she knew with a gaiety which some foreign visitors thought shockingly informal. While anxious officials put the finishing touches to the banquet, she changed into a violet velvet gown and took her place at the top table, under her cloth of state. Her great-uncle, Lord William Howard, and the Earl of Sussex served her on bended knee and trumpeters sounded each time a new course was carried in. There were masques and entertainments, music played and the banquet lasted until one o'clock in the morning. It was not surprising that the joust planned for the following day had to be post-poned, 'Her Majesty feeling rather tired'.

The weather on coronation day had been frosty, with some snow on the ground, and Elizabeth caught a heavy cold. As a result, her first parliament

57. The Anointing Spoon dates from the twelfth century and was used at Elizabeth I's coronation. The regalia itself disappeared during the Civil War and had to be replaced at the Restoration in 1660.
(Crown copyright)

had to be postponed briefly, but on 25 January she returned to Westminster for the opening, dazzling the spectators in a crimson robe lined with ermine, a cap of beaten gold studded with pearls on her hair and a magnificent pendant hung round her neck.

Even so, her temper was not of the best. The opening ceremony was always preceded by a Mass, and waiting at the abbey door was the Abbot himself, in pontifical vestments, with a procession of monks carrying torches. Elizabeth greeted the Abbot civilly enough, but when she noticed his companions, she snapped, 'Away with those torches, for we see very well', and she stalked up the aisle to her place. She loved elaborate ceremonial, rich vestments and beautiful church music, but she abhorred incense, Latin services and long sermons.

On this occasion the sermon was long enough. Dr Cox, recently returned

58. The Coronation Chair dates from about 1300 and was covered with cloth of silver for the coronation of Elizabeth I.
(By courtesy of the Dean and Chapter of Westminster: photograph, Jarrold Publishing)

from exile, inveighed against Roman Catholicism for an hour and a half, to the exasperation not only of the Queen but of the peers, who had to remain standing. There were sighs of relief all round when the service ended and they were able to move on to the House of Lords, where they sank gladly down on their benches and the Queen sat on her throne with its cloth of gold cushions.

For Elizabeth, parliament was a tiresome necessity. She believed that she had been chosen by God to rule England, and so she knew better than anyone else what should be done. She was willing to consult her expert advisers, of course, but no one was going to tell her what to do. The structure of society was, in her opinion, strictly hierarchical. Everyone had his appointed place, and hers was at the top. Her peers, assembled in the House of Lords, should provide the mechanism of legislation but the House of Commons was only there to vote her the revenues she needed.

Needless to say, parliament did not quite share her perception of the universe. Many of the members of her first parliament were enthusiastic Protestant supporters of her rule, but they were not going to sit meekly voting her supplies and waiting for her orders. On the contrary, they were playing an increasing part in initiating legislation and before they agreed to discuss anything else they made the Queen a solemn address urging her to marry and provide an heir. Their own lives depended on the continuance of Protestant rule.

Elizabeth was annoyed, but her reply was courteous, if firm. She had always resisted her sister's attempts to make her marry, she said, even when marriage had seemed the only way of avoiding death. If she had thought that parliament was trying to give her orders, she went on, she would have been much offended. However, as it was, she thanked them for their concern and assured them that she would never take a husband prejudicial to their interests. That said, she still believed that the single state was best, and 'this shall be for me sufficient, that a marble stone shall declare that a Queen, having reigned such a time, lived and died a virgin'. The House of Commons did not like it, but there was nothing they could do. They could only console themselves with the thought that she was young, healthy and attractive. Surely she would change her mind.

Someone else was particularly anxious about Elizabeth's matrimonial intentions: Philip of Spain. After his tedious years tied to Mary he had no desire to repeat the experience, but he had the sinking feeling that, for the sake of Europe's stability, he ought to marry the Queen of England himself. Elizabeth was very different from her sister, he knew. She was young, haughty and full of energy but apart from her tiresome manner she had one major drawback: she was a heretic. Would he be ruining his own reputation as a faithful son of the Church if he made her his third wife?

Never one to reach a decision quickly, he pondered for days until at last, in early January, he made up his mind. 'I have decided', he wrote to the Count de Feria, 'to place on one side all other considerations which might be urged against it, and am resolved to render this service to God and offer to marry the Queen of England'. She would have to become a Roman Catholic before he did so, of course, for 'In this way it will be evident and manifest that I am serving the Lord in marrying her and that she has been converted by my act'.

As soon as he received this cheering news, Feria hurried off to see Elizabeth and put the proposal. She listened in silence while he solemnly announced

59. *Henry II of France* by F Clouet. (Bibliothèque Nationale, Paris)

that his master was graciously willing to marry her and then, instead of leaping at the chance or even expressing humble gratitude, she launched into one of her usual complicated speeches about the virtues of virginity. Exasperated, he lost his diplomatic composure and suggested that if she did not marry and have an heir, their common enemy the King of France would put his own candidate on the English throne instead of her.

That was a mistake. Elizabeth flew into a tantrum and 'began to rave' against Henry II, his son, his daughter-in-law, the French, the Scots and everyone else. In fact, she stormed and raged for so long that in the end she had to sink down on a chair, exhausted, instead of maintaining her usual upright stance. The Count had touched a raw nerve. For centuries, France had been the enemy of England but the friend of Scotland. Whenever the English invaded France, they expected the Scots to retaliate by marching into England. Similarly, if England attacked the Scots, the French were supposed to come to the rescue. It did not always work out like that in practice, but the threat from the north was always there.

The situation had worsened considerably in recent years. The monarch of Scotland was a young girl and her subjects had sent her to France to be brought up at the court of Henry II. Now Mary, Queen of Scots was actually engaged to Henry's eldest son. One day she would be Queen of France as well, and if she had a son he would inherit both countries. As if that were not bad enough, Mary had a strong claim to the English throne. Her grandmother, Margaret Tudor, had been Henry VIII's sister.

60. *Mary, Queen of Scots*, painted by an unknown artist about the time of her marriage to the Dauphin.
(Reproduced by gracious permission of Her Majesty The Queen)

Margaret and her descendants had been ruled out of the succession in Henry's will, but King Henry II of France was not worried about that. On the very day that Elizabeth came to the throne, he announced that as a bastard she had no right to be there at all. His own daughter-in-law Mary was the real Queen of England. It was a diplomatic ploy, of course, but a dangerous one. Elizabeth was both furious and alarmed. From her early childhood she had suffered jeers about her so-called illegitimacy and she was profoundly sensitive about it. More to the point, Mary, Queen of Scots was a Roman Catholic, and it seemed all too likely that the Roman Catholics in England might rally to her cause.

The Count de Feria knew all that, of course, and it was precisely why he was implying that Elizabeth needed the help of a really powerful ally in the person of Philip II. He did not dare raise the question of his master's proposal again for some days, but when he did so, Elizabeth seemed more amenable. After a few innocuous conversations with her he even began to believe that she was beginning to come round to the notion. On 14 March, however, she told him flatly that the marriage could never take place because she was 'a heretic'. She and Philip could be friends, but nothing more.

Somewhat taken aback, the Count tried to ask her what had made her reach this decision, but she became 'so disturbed and excited' that he tried to convince her that neither he nor Philip regarded her as being a heretic. They were sure, he said, that she would never sanction the changes which were currently being discussed in parliament. Implying that, like Philip, she was a good Roman Catholic, he said that if she altered the religion of her country she would be ruined. Philip would never contemplate separating himself from the true Church if he were in her circumstances and afraid of losing his throne. He would not change his religion for all the kingdoms in the world. 'Then', retorted Elizabeth sourly, 'much less would he do it for a woman'. She had returned to the marriage question again. She was a Protestant and she would not convert to marry him, any more than he would become a heretic to marry her.

'Men', replied the Count urbanely, 'did more for a woman than for anything else', but he could see that she was scarcely listening to him. She was off on the subject of her religious settlement. Instead of quietly passing the Supremacy Bill severing England's ties with Rome again, her parliament seemed bent on making sweeping doctrinal changes. The members had even objected to her taking the title of Supreme Head of the Church of England,

61. *Matthew Parker*, Elizabeth's first Archbishop of Canterbury, by an unknown artist. They did not always agree and, disliking married clergy, the Queen was rude to his wife.
(Reproduced by kind permission of His Grace the Archbishop of Canterbury; copyright reserved to the Church Commissioners: photograph, Courtauld Institute of Art)

as her father and her brother had done. No sooner had that issue been raised in the House of Lords than the Bishop of Winchester had been on his feet, insolently reminding everyone of St Paul's ill-chosen remarks about no female being eligible to act as an apostle, a shepherd, a doctor or a preacher. That being so, the Bishop had proceeded, even more impertinently, how could a woman be Head of the Church?

Elizabeth recounted all this to Feria, telling him that she was perfectly willing to be called Supreme Governor instead. When she reached her favourite theme, 'that Bishops were lazy poltroons', the Count knew that he would get no further with Philip's marriage plan. Beating a hasty retreat to his lodgings, he sent the bad news to Brussels, where his King was staying. Philip was mightily relieved. 'Although I cannot help being sorry that the affair has not been arranged as public weal demanded', he replied in his usual ponderous way, 'yet as the Queen thinks it was not necessary, and that with good friendship we shall attain the same subject, I am content that it should be so.'

That spring, Spain, France, England and Scotland signed a treaty of peace at Cateau-Cambrésis. Elizabeth did not manage to get Calais back, but although its loss was a humiliation it was also a relief, for it would have been a great financial burden. Another clause in the treaty stated that Philip II would marry Henry II's eldest daughter Elisabeth, a pretty young girl of thirteen. The Count de Feria was given the unenviable task of breaking this news to Elizabeth but, to his surprise, when he went to tell her she was looking reasonably pleasant. Indeed, before he could utter a word of his carefully-rehearsed speech, she smiled and said sweetly that she had heard that His Majesty was to take a wife. He gave a cautious reply and even as he spoke he heard her give 'little sighs, which bordered upon laughter'.

Looking at her suspiciously, he remarked that he was sorry she had not married Philip herself. That, she replied, was the King of Spain's own fault, not hers, and she added pensively that Philip could not have been as deeply in love with her as Feria would have had her believe, since he 'had not had patience to wait four months for her'. Squirming under her bright, alert gaze, the Count once again had the uncomfortable feeling that she was laughing at him.

62. *Princess Elisabeth of France*, third wife of Philip II of Spain, by an unknown artist. (Bibliothèque Nationale, Paris)

5

LORD ROBERT

THE WEDDING of Philip II and Princess Elisabeth had an unexpectedly tragic consequence. Philip did not go to France in person for his third venture into matrimony, but the proxy wedding was held with much magnificence and there were elaborate celebrations afterwards. An enthusiastic jouster, Henry II arranged a series of tournaments in which he himself was a leading contender. The third time he rode in the lists he suffered a fatal accident. His opponent's lance shattered, and splinters lodged in the King's eye. Ten days later he died and the Dauphin and Mary, Queen of Scots became King and Queen of France.

There was little to be feared from the new Francis II. A dull, sullen teenager, he was totally dominated by his crafty mother, Catherine de Medici, but his wife and her Guise relatives were a different matter. Whether of her own volition or at their prompting, Mary called herself Queen of England and used the English royal arms. They appeared on her canopy of state, her banners and her silver plate.

The English were relying upon the Treaty of Cateau-Cambrésis to remedy that, and throughout the summer, Elizabeth was in a high good humour. She had dissolved parliament after legislation settling the church, she had no need to worry any further about the expense of war with France and she did not have to suffer the unwelcome attentions of Philip II as a suitor. There were others eager to put marriage proposals, of course, the most eligible being Prince Eric of Sweden and the Archdukes Ferdinand and Charles of the Holy Roman Empire. It entertained her to hear their envoys describe how handsome, how brave and how deeply devoted to her these strangers were and it was useful, too, for it encouraged her own subjects to believe that she was seriously contemplating matrimony. In fact, she was in no mood to give

63. *Archduke Charles of Austria* by an unknown artist.
(Kunsthistorisches Museum, Vienna)

64. *Francis II of France*, husband of Mary, Queen of Scots, seen in an enamel attributed to Leonard Limosin I.
(Scottish National Portrait Gallery)

serious thought to anything. After the momentous events of the past year she
needed some relaxation, and with the coming of the good weather she began
to spend long days out of doors, hunting, in company with her Master of the
Horse.

Privy Council meetings and state papers were ignored. When she returned
in the evening she was all too often to be found laughing and flirting with
Lord Robert Dudley in quiet corners, in window embrasures, or in crowded
galleries. She was excited, animated, at her teasing worst and already gossip
was flying round the court. She was in love with Robert, people whispered;
she was his mistress, she was pregnant with his child. The rumours would
become a major scandal if something were not done, but when Cecil tried to
hint that she should moderate her behaviour, be more discreet, she only
laughed and turned back to her friend.

What lay between Elizabeth and Lord Robert, the traitor's son, 'the Gypsy',
with the black hair and the dark, alluring glance? Their contemporaries specu-
lated endlessly and historians have argued about it ever since. Could the
Virgin Queen really have taken a lover or was she peculiarly immune to
masculine charms, frigid, psychologically damaged by her strange childhood,
perhaps even physically malformed? It is impossible, of course, to find evidence of anything as intimate after the passage of four hundred years, but
there is no evidence to suggest that she was incapable of childbearing. The
foreign ambassadors at court had spies throughout her household, and particularly when their masters thought of marrying her they questioned everyone, even her laundresses, for signs of anything unusual.

The reports they sent back were reassuring. The Queen menstruated regularly and as she was healthy and active there was no reason to suppose that
she could not bear sons. William Cecil and her other ministers made the same
assumption. When she was well into her forties they were worrying about
the danger to her life should she take their advice at last, marry and bear
children. Assuming that they were not misled, the danger of pregnancy may
well have played its part in restraining her from giving herself to Robert.

That apart, what of her psychological and emotional attitude? Much non-sense has been written about Elizabeth the neurotic, the poor, innocent child brought up by a monster of a father who murdered his wives. There is no denying that the events of her childhood were traumatic and they may well have given her a lasting sense of insecurity, but the conventions of the six-teenth century were rather different from those of the twentieth. Elizabeth, Mary Tudor, Henry VIII, Mary, Queen of Scots and all the other monarchs of the day accepted that miscreants must be punished, and that the punishment for traitors was death.

Kings and queens were chosen by God to preserve the natural order of the world, and if keeping that order meant authorising the execution of friends and even relatives, then that was one of the burdens of power. The knowledge that her father was king had made his every act, however unreasonable, seem acceptable, and by the same token her sense of her own majesty set her apart from everyone else and rendered even the most attractive young man someone with whom she could never have an intimate relationship unless he was royal.

If it had not been for that, her friendship with Robert might have ended differently, for they had much in common. She was only a few months

67. Medieval gittern given by Elizabeth to Lord Robert.
(Reproduced by courtesy of the Trustees of the British Museum)

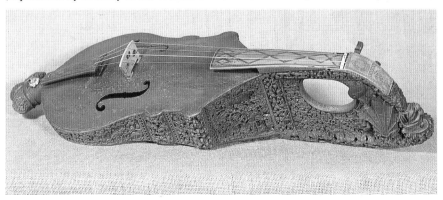

younger than he, and they had known each other since they were eight years old. Both Robert and she had Roger Ascham as a tutor, although not at the same time. When Robert eventually gave up his Latin and Greek in favour of mathematics, 'You did yourself injury in changing Tully's wisdom with Euclid's pricks and lines', Roger told him reproachfully. The decision was probably made because his father, the Duke of Northumberland, foresaw a military career for his fifth son. Robert would not inherit the family titles. He would have to make his own way in the world.

He gained military experience early, for when he was sixteen his father sent him to put down Kett's rebellion in Norfolk, and, when the Duke tried to make Lady Jane Grey queen, Robert rode with him to East Anglia in pursuit of Mary Tudor. He was captured after a week or two and sent to the Tower. Although Elizabeth and he could not have seen each other during their months of incarceration, shared adversity must have drawn them closer. In the end, Philip II's intervention secured Robert's release as well as hers, and after a period of exile on the continent he came back home and was often to be found at Hatfield or Ashridge during the last months of Mary's reign.

He and Elizabeth were without doubt sexually attracted to each other. Later encounters showed that he always gravitated towards thin, vivacious redheads while she preferred tall, handsome, magnificently dressed, athletic men like Thomas Seymour and her own father. Robert possessed all the necessary attributes. In addition, they both had quick, darting minds, a down to earth approach to life and an irreverent sense of humour. Elizabeth was never sentimental, she had no patience with soulful, pompous people. She liked men of action, she said, not those who sat at home by the fire.

Soon, they were inseparable. His position required him to plan state ceremonial and organise processions. He was good at that. Like Elizabeth, he had a sense of drama and he loved theatricals. Already he had his own company of players. He also had an expert knowledge of horses, and it was he who selected those ridden by the Queen. Soon, he was undertaking a wide range of helpful, necessary tasks. Anyone wishing to speak to Her Majesty or seek her favour found it prudent to approach him first. He could arrange an audience, see that she read a petition, draw her attention to an eager supplicant – all in return for money, of course, for he had to finance his lavish way of life. In short, he took on the role of royal favourite and so useful was he in reporting everything to Elizabeth that she nicknamed him her 'Eyes'.

68. *Thomas Tallis*, Master of Music of Elizabeth's Chapel Royal, engraved by an unknown artist. (Reproduced by courtesy of the Trustees of the British Museum)

The booke of Hunting. 135

that the Prince or chiefe (if it so please them) doe alight and take
assaye of the Deare with a sharpe knyfe, the whiche is done
L.iij. iij

69. *Elizabeth I out hunting*, woodcut from *The booke of Hunting*. (The British Library)

William Cecil was jealous: everyone was. A favourite might be necessary to the monarch, but he had few friends and in Robert's case it was all too easy for people to recall that not only his father but his grandfather had been executed for treason. The Dudley blood was tainted. How could the Queen possibly trust him? The more envious the courtiers became, the more ready were they to believe the rumours about him, rumours which were all the more shocking because, as Elizabeth and everyone else knew, Lord Robert was a married man.

He himself may well have described to her how he had met Amy, the daughter of a Norfolk squire, during Kett's rebellion, had fallen in love with her and had married her. He had been seventeen, she eighteen. Ten years had passed since then, and in that time they had drifted apart. Amy was never seen at court. There was nothing unusual in that. Many wives stayed quietly at home, bringing up the children and running the family estates while their ambitious husbands sought preferment from the monarch. The few surviving scraps of Amy's correspondence suggest that she did look after some of his financial affairs for him and he certainly visited her from time to time, but they had no children and she was not running her own establishment. She always seemed to live with relatives or friends. Perhaps she was delicate, or suffering from depression. By 1559 there were rumours that she was seriously ill.

As far as Elizabeth was concerned, Amy was out of sight and also out of mind. Her own friendship with Katherine Parr had not prevented her from flirting with Lord Thomas Seymour when she was a girl and her awareness of Amy's existence did not affect her closeness to Robert. Everyone else, however, could see that the relationship was extremely damaging. Kings

70. *Elizabeth I* in about 1560, by an unknown artist.
(National Portrait Gallery, London)

might take mistresses, but unmarried queens were expected to be above reproach.

When Kate Ashley went down on her knees and told her so, Elizabeth simply laughed. It was ludicrous to suggest that she could have an illicit relationship with anyone, she said. She was surrounded by crowds of people all day long and at night her ladies were close at hand. How could she be

71. *Mary of Guise*, the Queen Regent of Scotland, by Corneille de Lyon.
(Scottish National Portrait Gallery)

any man's mistress? She was flattered by the notion rather than annoyed, but in typical manner she added defiantly 'If she had ever had the will or had found pleasure in such a dishonourable life – from which God preserve her – she did not know of anyone who could forbid her'. The Queen would do as she liked.

William Cecil was seriously disturbed. Alarming news from Scotland had arrived, but he seemed completely unable to get her to pay attention to it. Until now, that country had been kept under the allegiance of Rome by its Regent, Mary of Guise, mother of Mary, Queen of Scots. Now, there had been a Protestant uprising and the Regent had sent to France for help. Soldiers had arrived in Scotland and more were expected. Horrified at the thought that they might defeat the Protestants and then turn south against his own country, Cecil was determined to send assistance to the Scots, but he could do nothing without Elizabeth's permission.

He nagged and cajoled until finally she agreed to send a little money, but he could see that she did not like the idea. He was asking her to support rebels against their lawful monarch, she told him sharply, and refused to discuss the matter further. In the end, he had to threaten to resign before she would do anything more. 'With a sorrowful heart and watery eyes', he wrote, 'I, your poor servant and most lowly subject, an unworthy Secretary, beseech Your Majesty to pardon this, my lowly suit, that considering the proceeding in this matter for removing the French out of Scotland doth not content Your Majesty, and that I cannot with my conscience give any contrary advice I may, with Your Majesty's favour and clemency, be spared to intermeddle therein . . . And as for any other service, though it were in Your Majesty's kitchen or garden, from the bottom of my heart I am ready without respect of estimation, wealth or ease, to do Your Majesty's commandment to my life's end.'

72. 'Elizabeth dancing with Lord Robert Dudley at Penshurst Place', by an unknown artist. (Reproduced by permission of Viscount De L'Isle, from his private collection)

He did not mean it, of course, but it had the desired effect. The Queen agreed, grudgingly. The Protestants were officially led by the head of the house of Hamilton, although their most active member was Lord James Stewart, the illegitimate half-brother of Mary, Queen of Scots. By the Treaty of Berwick of 27 February 1560, Elizabeth promised to send help against the Regent. A small fleet sailed north and an English army began to besiege the French in Leith. Cecil was relieved, and after the death of Mary of Guise in June, peace negotiations were announced. His satisfaction was all too brief, however, for Elizabeth sent for him and told him that he must leave for Edinburgh at once. He was to be one of her chief negotiators. Full of dark suspicions that this was a plot by Lord Robert to get him out of the way, he rode north.

His mission was successful. By the Treaty of Edinburgh, all foreign soldiers, English and French, would leave Scotland and Elizabeth had insisted on a provision stating that Mary, Queen of Scots and her husband Francis would stop calling themselves King and Queen of England and would give up quartering the English royal arms with their own.

While the Scottish parliament passed legislation making their country officially Protestant, Cecil rode proudly back to London, expecting a joyful welcome from his mistress, congratulations, perhaps even a celebratory banquet. Instead, her greeting was perfunctory and before long she had worked herself up into a rage because he had not secured the return of Calais. Lord Robert Dudley had obviously been at work, denigrating all his efforts, and he was in despair.

On 6 September 1560, a new Spanish ambassador arrived at court to replace the Count de Feria. Alvarez de Quadra, Bishop of Aquila, travelled to Windsor to present his credentials and was invited to stay for a few days. The very next afternoon he was startled when the Queen came back from hunting and told him that Lord Robert's wife was 'dead, or nearly so, and begged me to say nothing about it'. This was riveting news. Needless to say, he had heard all about Elizabeth's relationship with Robert from his predecessor, and he was in a fever of suspense. If Amy Robsart died, would she marry him?

He was not alone in his concern. William Cecil was terrified that Elizabeth would do just that. He dared not approach her directly about her intentions, but someone had to intervene and point out the dangers of what she was doing. Casting around desperately, he decided to enlist the help of Bishop de Quadra. On the evening of 8 September, he made his way to the ambassador's lodgings and asked to see him. Eager to hear of any new development, the Bishop welcomed him gladly and listened with surprise as the usually urbane secretary poured out his fears. He was at the end of his tether, he said. Lord Robert was all-powerful at court and Elizabeth was entirely under his influence. He had decided to resign.

When the Bishop expressed astonishment and disbelief, Cecil declared that it was a poor sailor who did not make for port when he saw a storm coming. Disaster lay ahead, 'for he himself perceived the most manifest ruin impending over the Queen through her intimacy with Lord Robert. The Lord Robert had made himself master of the business of the state and of the person of the Queen, to the extreme injury of the realm, with the intention of marrying her'. He begged de Quadra to speak to Elizabeth and tell her 'not utterly to throw herself away as she was doing, and to remember what she owed to herself and her subjects'.

According to Quadra's description of their conversation, Cecil went even further. He said twice that Lord Robert would be better in paradise than on earth, and as a grand climax he confided that the pair were thinking of destroying Robert's wife, who was not really ill at all. De Quadra was bewildered. Everybody knew that Amy was ill. Everybody also knew that Cecil was Elizabeth's most loyal servant. What did it mean?

The most likely explanation is that the Cecil was trying in every way possible to prevent the Queen from marrying the wrong man. He was aware that Quadra's intervention might not work. Elizabeth might allow the Bishop to broach the subject because he was a new ambassador and she would not expect him to start speaking about it, but she would all too probably cut him short and send him packing. Cecil therefore needed a second, more devious plan.

He realised all too well how deeply attached the Queen was to Robert and he knew that she would be seriously tempted to marry him if he were free. That might happen at any moment, for Amy was by all accounts terminally ill with cancer of the breast. That accounted for Elizabeth's air of suppressed excitement. There was only one way to stop her altogether and that was to convince her that people were saying that she and Robert had plotted Amy's death. No matter how much she was in love with Robert, she would never risk her reputation by marrying him in those circumstances.

At the end of that long and strange evening the Bishop of Aquila was bewildered, but Cecil went home feeling slightly easier in his mind. One way or another, he had surely set in motion the means of preventing the Queen from taking a rash, ambitious husband who would ruin them all.

Was his strange tale inspired by the knowledge that Amy Robsart had died mysteriously that very same day? For the past few weeks she had been staying at Cumnor Hall, a house rented by her husband on a short lease. Interestingly enough, its owner was Dr Owen, one of the Queen's favourite medical advisers, and Mrs Owen was staying there with Amy. Also in the house were Mrs John Oddingsells, Amy's companion, Lord Robert's Treasurer, Antony Foster, and his wife. Mrs Foster was the niece of Elizabeth's old friend Lord Williams of Thame. A few historians have insinuated that there was something sinister in this ménage, but it does sound more like a comfortable arrangement for a young woman who was seriously ill.

Lord Robert was at court on Sunday, 8 September, and when Amy rose she surprised her companions by ordering them to go to the local fair. Mrs Oddingsells was unwilling. All the ordinary people went on a Sunday, she said, and she had no desire to mingle with the crowd. Amy was very angry with them. She scolded them and shouted at them and in the end she said that Mrs Oddingsells could go when she chose but all the servants must attend that morning. She then arranged to dine at eleven o'clock with Mrs Owen. She was never seen alive again.

Cumnor Hall was a rambling mansion, built round a courtyard, and presumably the occupants had rooms in different wings. At any rate, it was not until the servants came back from the fair in the afternoon that they found Amy lying at the foot of a flight of stairs. There were no marks of violence on her. Indeed, her cap was hardly disturbed, but her neck was broken.

There is no reason why Cecil could not have learned that very night what had happened, but officially the news did not reach London until the following day. When Lord Robert was told, he was appalled. His enemies had been saying for months that he was trying to poison Amy. Now he would be

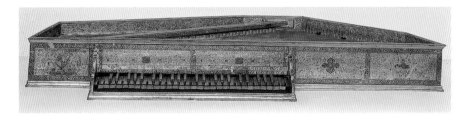

73. Virginal belonging to Queen Elizabeth. The Italian-made case has the arms of the Boleyn family.
(By courtesy of the Board of Trustees of the Victoria and Albert Museum)

accused of sending someone to push her down the stairs. 'The greatness and suddenness of the misfortune doth so perplex me, until I do hear from you how the matter standeth or how this evil doth light upon me, considering what the malicious world will bruit [say], as I can take no rest', he wrote to his kinsman Thomas Blount, begging for further details.

Elizabeth realised the implications too. Just when the way had seemed clear for them, this evil stroke of fortune had ruined everything. Robert could not remain at court with this dreadful cloud of suspicion hanging over him, so she told him to go to his house at Kew and stay there until she allowed him to return. He did not want to go, of course, and he was terrified that she might listen to his enemies and banish him permanently, but he had no choice in the matter.

He was desperate for an inquest to exonerate him, presumably by finding the real culprit, for he seemed genuinely to believe that his wife had been murdered. The jury brought in a different verdict. Death by misadventure

74. The Greenwich armour of Lord Robert Dudley, Earl of Leicester, about 1575. Originally the bands were gilt and the surfaces blued or russeted.
(The Board of Trustees of the Royal Armouries)

75. Windsor Castle, visited by Elizabeth on her summer progress in 1567: seen from the River Thames.
(A F Kersting)

was their conclusion. They had thought that Amy might have committed suicide, for her maid had said unthinkingly, 'I myself have heard her pray to God to deliver her from desperation', but the woman swiftly denied any such meaning when it was put to her. How had her mistress died, then, she was asked. 'By my faith, I do judge very chance, and neither done by man nor by herself,' she answered. Amy had been a God-fearing woman, and she would never have made away with herself.

From Lord Robert's point of view, the verdict was highly unsatisfactory, for it did not clear him. Whatever the official opinion, many people in England and everyone in France believed that it was murder and most of them thought that he had planned the crime. The official transcript of the inquest's proceedings has long since disappeared, as have Lord Robert's letters to his cousin Blount, and learned articles, historical works and novels have all propounded different theories about the so-called crime. In recent years, however, the jury's verdict has received support from expert medical opinion.

In 1956, Professor Ian Aird examined the medical findings contained in the surviving documents and he came to an interesting conclusion. Suicides do not

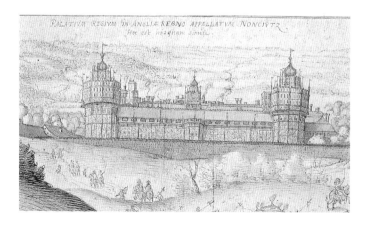

76. The palace of Nonsuch, a favourite royal residence. (Photograph, Picturepoint–London)

throw themselves down staircases, he said, particularly the shallow staircase of a Tudor house. They look for something far higher, like a tower or a cliff. As for murder, there were no signs of violence on the corpse. He therefore returned to the possibility of natural causes.

There are two illnesses which can result in a spontaneous fracture of the vertebrae, he observed. One is tuberculosis, but no one ever mentioned that Amy had consumption or suffered from a cough or any of the other serious symptoms of the disease. The other illness is cancer of the breast. The malignant cells produced can result in softening of the bone, and a spontaneous fracture of the neck might have occurred if Amy had tripped on the stairs. Since it was already known that she had been suffering from a 'malady of the breast', Professor Aird concluded that this was the most likely cause of her death.

His arguments are convincing and he may well have uncovered the truth but, natural or unnatural, her death in suspicious circumstances had the same effect. 'The Queen of England is going to marry her horsekeeper, who has killed his wife to make room for her', Mary, Queen of Scots jeered, with a little laugh, and her sentiments were echoed throughout Europe. English ambassadors abroad wrote home in desperation warning that Elizabeth would be ruined forever if she married Robert now.

The Queen herself was obviously in the grip of conflicting emotions. In October, she assured Quadra that she had decided not to marry Lord Robert or anyone else, but he noticed that she was looking pale and depressed. Cecil, on the other hand, seemed extremely cheerful and he bustled off to Kew to offer consolation to his disgraced rival. He spoke to him in such a friendly manner, all former enmity apparently forgotten, that Robert was pathetically grateful and wrote him a note to say so.

Whatever Cecil's motives in going to Kew, he would hardly have done so without royal approval. It was an encouraging sign and, sure enough, Robert was allowed back again before long. Soon, he and Elizabeth seemed as close as ever. On Midsummer Day, for instance, they attended a water pageant together on the River Thames. The Queen invited Quadra aboard the royal barge to view the spectacle and soon she and Robert were busy enjoying their favourite sport of baiting the Spanish ambassador. Robert gaily suggested that 'if she liked' the Bishop could marry the pair of them there and then. Keeping a straight face Elizabeth replied that she was not sure if Quadra knew enough English for the purpose. The Bishop was half inclined to believe that they were in earnest, although he knew very well her love of banter. She was always joking, he noted sourly, 'which she likes to do much better than talking about business'. All the same, he thought it worth reporting the incident word for word to Philip II in case there was anything in it.

Robert, in fact, was still hoping that in spite of the Amy Robsart scandal he could become the Queen's husband. He went around telling people that if she married anyone it would be him, and he nagged at her constantly to give him a peerage so that there would not be such a discrepancy in status between them. For reasons of her own, she finally agreed to the title and her lawyers drew up documents creating him Earl of Leicester. However, when the charter was placed before her, instead of picking up the pen and writing her name, she seized a knife and slashed the parchment from side to side in a gesture of bitterness and rage. If marriage to Robert had been possible she would probably have rejected him, but now that she could not have him he was what she wanted most in life.

77. Lord Robert's sister, *Lady Mary Sidney*, who nursed Elizabeth through smallpox, caught the disease and was dreadfully disfigured. Hans Eworth painted this portrait earlier.
(National Trust, at Petworth: photograph, Courtauld Institute of Art)

The nearest she ever came to expressing her true feelings for him was in October 1562 when she fell seriously ill. The German Dr Burcot, summoned to examine her, diagnosed smallpox, whereupon she promptly had him thrown out. She had a high fever, and her condition deteriorated rapidly after that until she lapsed into a coma. Her distraught privy councillors gathered round her bedside, discussing in agitated undertones the awful crisis which loomed before them. What were they to do if she died? They could not agree who should succeed her. Some wanted Lady Jane Grey's sister Catherine, some favoured the Countess of Lennox and others preferred the Earl of Huntingdon.

Before they could reach any decision, the Queen suddenly opened her eyes and seemed about to speak. Eagerly, they leaned over her, straining to hear what she would say. If she died, she whispered, she wanted Robert to be Lord Protector of England, and they would have to give him £20,000 a year so that he could live in the proper state. Perhaps observing their horrified expressions, she added that although she had always loved him dearly, as God was her witness, nothing improper had ever passed between them. Exhausted by the effort of talking, she fell back on her pillows and drifted into a peaceful sleep. From that moment she began to recover and, to their immeasurable relief, her councillors realised that Lord Robert was not to be their master after all.

6

MARY, QUEEN OF SCOTS

THROUGHOUT THE DRAMAS of the Amy Robsart crisis, Elizabeth was uneasily aware that the Scottish problem was not yet settled. The French had glibly promised that Mary, Queen of Scots would give up using the English royal title and arms, but neither she nor her husband had yet ratified the Treaty of Edinburgh and Elizabeth was rapidly becoming convinced that they never would.

She was also irritated by the glowing reports she kept hearing of Mary herself. Seventeen years old and nearly six feet tall, the girl was apparently a beauty and the poets of the French court seemed to have nothing better to do than rhapsodise over her creamy skin, her auburn hair, her narrow brown eyes, her elegance and her grace. Worse still, English visitors to France were equally bewitched by her charm and they came back full of stories of her gentleness, her femininity and her wit. Some even seemed to be hinting that outspoken, uninhibited Elizabeth would do well to learn from her cousin's more decorous behaviour.

There was trouble ahead, Elizabeth felt sure, but when it came it took an unexpected form. In November 1560, Mary's husband Francis II developed an ear infection, a high fever and delirium. A few weeks later, he was dead.

78. *Mary, Queen of Scots* in white mourning after the death of her first husband, Francis II, by an unknown artist. (Reproduced by gracious permission of Her Majesty The Queen)

THES BE THE SONES OF TF RIGHT HONERABLES 'FEFLLE OF LENOXE AD
'TE LADY MARGARETZ GRACE, COVNTYES OF LENOXE AD ANGWYSE.

CHARLLES STEWARDE
HIS BROTHER, ÆTATIS, 6.

HENRY STEWARDE, LORD DAR-
LEY AND DOWGLAS, ÆTATIS, 17

79. *Henry, Lord Darnley* at the
age of seventeen, with his six-
year-old brother Charles,
painted by Eworth, probably for
their mother.
(Reproduced by gracious
permission of Her Majesty The
Queen)

This made little difference to the government of France since his mother
Catherine de Medici would go on ruling the country on behalf of her next
son, Charles IX, but it did raise one perplexing question. What would Mary,
Queen of Scots do next?

Elizabeth and Cecil would have liked to think that she would remain where
she was, merging meekly into the background as Queen Dowager of France,
but that hardly seemed probable. Everyone knew that Mary and her mother-
in-law did not get on. There was little prospect of her taking second place to
Catherine de Medici. She was much more likely to look for another husband.

Sure enough, long before the widow's official month of mourning was over,
she was having discussions with the Spaniards, and the reason soon became
clear. She had set her heart on marrying Philip II's son Carlos, Elizabeth's
former suitor. A queen from the time she was six days old, Mary said quite
openly that she could never consider taking a husband of lesser status. Her
consort would have to be a king or a king's son.

Deeply concerned, Elizabeth decided to send an emissary to find out what
was really going on. The Earl of Bedford, an upright Protestant gentleman,
would surely be immune to Mary's charms and so he was dispatched to France
with instructions to discover all he could about her intentions, under the
pretext of offering Elizabeth's condolences on the death of Francis.

The Earl duly rode to Fontainebleau, where the French court was staying,
and gained admittance to the Queen of Scots. He was immediately impressed.
She saw him almost alone, with only her ladies-in-waiting for company, and

she spoke to him in a friendly, confiding way. Of course she was anxious for Elizabeth's goodwill, she said. After all, they were 'both in one isle, both of one language, both the nearest kinswoman that each other hath, and both Queens'.

She turned aside his questions with a smile, asking sweetly for Elizabeth's portrait and speaking wistfully of her longing to meet the English Queen. When he asked her to ratify the Treaty of Edinburgh, she sighed and told him softly that she could do nothing until she had spoken to her advisers . . . who were, of course, in Scotland. Only afterwards, composing his report for Elizabeth, did he realise the embarrassing truth. He had learned nothing from the conversation at all.

Soon after his visit, another protagonist in the unfolding drama made his way to Fontainebleau. This was a pretty, fourteen-year-old boy with a round, innocent face and fair curly hair. Henry, Lord Darnley, was the elder son of that inveterate schemer, the Countess of Lennox. Since the days when Mary Tudor had seemed to be promoting her as heir to the throne, the Countess had been busy with all sorts of projects, some of which resulted in Elizabeth imprisoning her in the Tower of London from time to time. The Queen liked her, however, and after her various Roman Catholic plots she was always restored to favour again.

Lady Lennox's ambitions on her own behalf had by now faded, for all her attention was concentrated on her first and favourite son. Lord Darnley was the great grandson of Henry VII, and she had named him after his Tudor forbears. She was having him carefully educated in all the courtly skills, and she dreamed of a marvellous future for him. If he only could marry his cousin, Mary, Queen of Scots, their claims to the English throne would be united and they would have a very good chance of making them a reality.

80. *Charles IX of France*, soon after becoming King, by François Clouet.
(Bibliothèque Nationale, Paris)

Mary had met the boy once, when he went over to France at the time of her husband's coronation. He had received a formal welcome, little more. This time it could be different. Mary was free, and Henry, if not exactly a man, was certainly no longer a child. His mother therefore resolved to send him across again at once, to offer her condolences to her bereaved niece.

Elizabeth's permission was necessary, and she gave it, perhaps in an unguarded moment, perhaps because she surmised that Mary was far too taken up with her Spanish machinations to pay attention to a callow youth who was a mere earl's son. If this was her belief, she was correct. Nothing immediate came of the encounter, but the Countess of Lennox did not despair. There was time yet, for by all accounts Catherine de Medici was about to prevent Mary from marrying Don Carlos. When Mary realised that she would have to look for a husband elswhere, the Countess and her son would be ready.

Reports that the Spanish match was foundering pleased Elizabeth in one way, but at the same time they alarmed her. If she could not have Don Carlos, the Queen of Scots might return to her own kingdom to disturb the newly-settled Protestant government of her brother, Lord James. Needless to say, he relished this prospect no more than Elizabeth did and he too decided to go to France to see Mary. Instead of taking the sea route, he set off overland, so that he could call in at London and consult his old friend, William Cecil.

After anxious discussions together, Cecil took him to see Elizabeth. Lord James was just two years older than she was, and, like her, he was a direct descendant of Henry VII. He was an impressive figure, a dark-haired, strong-ly-built man with a considerable presence. One of the many illegitimate sons of King James V of Scotland, he had a distinctly regal manner and the English thought him well-fitted to be a king. Indeed, Cecil and his colleagues deeply regretted that an accident of birth had deprived this reliable Protestant of the

Scottish throne. How much simpler everything would have been if he had inherited his father's crown instead of Mary. There were those who said that Lord James fully subscribed to this view himself, but if he did, he hid his feelings very well and usually exhibited only a proper concern for the future of his country and its Reformed Church.

Elizabeth was not really interested in the ramifications of the ecclesiastical settlement in Scotland. Her thoughts were all on Mary and her intentions. Lord James did not know what these were any more than she did, of course, but they talked together about what might happen in Scotland and Lord James finally went on his way, muttering about trying to convert Mary to Protestantism. That proved impossible. She listened politely to him and then suggested that if he would convert to Roman Catholicism she could have him made a cardinal. He declined, and they finally agreed that she should return to her native land on the understanding that she could worship as she pleased but that she would not interfere with the Protestant church.

In July 1561 her emissary, the Seigneur D'Oysel, arrived in England and was ushered into Elizabeth's presence. He had come to seek a safe conduct for Mary, he explained. She was about to set sail for Scotland and she wanted to ensure that if storms blew her ashore in England she would be allowed to travel on unmolested. Elizabeth fixed him with a beady eye, heard him out and then asked him curtly whether Mary had now ratified the Treaty of Edinburgh. There was an embarrassed silence. Finally, Monsieur D'Oysel admitted that she had not yet done so. In that case, snapped Elizabeth, there could be no safe conduct.

Monsieur D'Oysel was shocked at this startling breach of diplomatic etiquette. So was Mary, but she was determined not to let it stand in her way and on 14 August 1561 she sailed from Calais. Elizabeth's fleet followed her galleys for a time and they even searched her baggage vessels on the pretext of looking for pirates, but she reached Scotland safely on 19 August.

To everyone's surprise, she received a rapturous welcome and soon settled

82. Temple Newsam House, Yorkshire home of Lord and Lady Lennox, where Darnley was brought up. The west wing is early sixteenth-century, the other parts seventeenth-century.
(Leeds City Art Galleries: Temple Newsam House)

down to rule with moderation and considerable statesmanship, advised by
Lord James and William Maitland of Lethington, a subtle politician who was
Scotland's nearest equivalent to William Cecil. Before long, Elizabeth began
to receive cordial letters from her but there was an insuperable obstacle to any
real friendship between them. Mary had declared that she could not ratify the
Treaty of Edinburgh until Elizabeth recognised her publicly as heir to the
English throne, and that Elizabeth declined to do.

She told Maitland bluntly when he came to see her that 'So long as I live I
shall be Queen of England. When I am dead, they shall succeed me who have
the most right . . .' It was unreasonable 'to require me in mine own life to set
my winding sheet before my eyes. I know the inconstancy of the English
people', she went on, 'how they ever mislike the present government and
have their eyes fixed upon that person who is next to succeed', and she
concluded by quoting a Latin epigram: 'More people adore the rising sun than
the setting sun!' As soon as she nominated the Queen of Scots there would
be one plot after another and she would have no peace.

She was careful not to say who she believed had the best claim to her
throne, but Lord Robert and William Cecil both assured Maitland that she
favoured Mary, the senior heir in the female line. If only the Queen of Scots
would accept this and stop pressing for public recognition, they could coexist
perfectly well, but as Maitland had already remarked, 'The Queen my Mistress
is descended of the Blood of England and so of the race of the Lion on both
sides. I fear she could rather be content to hazard all, such is her courage,
than receive that dishonour to forego her right'. There was little hope of
compromise. Elizabeth and Mary went on corresponding, they exchanged
valuable gifts and they spoke enthusiastically of a personal meeting, but they

remained highly suspicious of each other and when it came to the point Elizabeth always found a good reason for postponing the encounter.

She was still much concerned about Mary's marriage plans, and early in 1563 a number of worrying rumours circulated in London. Most people were saying that the Queen of Scots would marry the Holy Roman Emperor's son, the Archduke Charles, but those who really knew had a different theory. Charles was not nearly important enough for her, they said. They had heard that she was secretly reviving her scheme to marry Don Carlos. If that were so, she would have to be stopped.

Elizabeth was aware that a stern warning would not be enough. She had learned from experience that opposition would make Mary more obstinate than ever. Some diversionary tactic was needed, some rival claimant who would take up her interest, keep her occupied for months to come in fruitless negotiation. Elizabeth was not in a position to persuade a foreign prince to take on this role, and in any event that would be too risky. An ambitious man might be tempted to go ahead and marry the Queen of Scots. No, the candidate would have to be someone whom Elizabeth could control: someone she could trust. Suddenly, she thought of the very person.

In March 1563, when Maitland was in London yet again, she summoned him to her presence and remarked airily that she was prepared to offer his Queen a husband 'in whom nature has implanted so many graces that if *she* wished to marry, she would prefer him to all other princes in the world'. She mentioned no names, but after a moment's bafflement Maitland realised that she was referring to none other than Lord Robert Dudley.

Mary's secretary could hardly believe his ears. Could she really be offering his virtuous Queen this traitor's son, this wife-murderer, her own lover? It seemed incredible. He was, however, too experienced a diplomat to reveal his outrage and he told Elizabeth suavely, 'This was a great proof of the love she bore his Queen, that she was willing to give her a thing so dearly prized by herself'. However, he went on, Mary would not wish to deprive her cousin of 'all the joy and solace she received from his company'. Far from taking offence at the innuendo, Elizabeth laughed appreciatively and replied that it was a pity Lord Robert's brother was not as handsome and as graceful as he was. If he had been, she and Mary could each have married a member of the Dudley family.

Maitland hoped that the whole distasteful incident could be passed off as a joke, but in June 1563 she returned to the attack. If Mary were to marry Don Carlos, the Archduke Charles or any other relative of the Holy Roman Emperor, she would make Elizabeth her enemy for life. If, on the other hand, she chose someone of whom the Queen of England approved, then Elizabeth would recognise her as heir to her throne. That surely would make the Queen of Scots take the matter seriously.

Even then, Mary remained indifferent to the suggestion. Her heart was still set on Don Carlos and she did not even bother to express indignation at the offer of the scandalous Lord Robert. Loath to abandon a good idea, Elizabeth continued to press the match, never mentioning Robert by name but dropping a series of very broad hints. Mary should choose 'some person of noble birth within our realm . . . yea perchance such as she should hardly think we could agree to . . .'

Her persistence finally bore fruit. The Don Carlos plan collapsed in August 1564, not because of anything Elizabeth did but because the boy had suffered brain damage in a fall and as a result was so mentally unstable that he was

84. *Margaret, Countess of Lennox,* in the 1570s, by an unknown artist. (Detail) (Reproduced by gracious permission of Her Majesty The Queen)

not fit to marry anyone. When Mary recovered from her initial disappointment, she began to see Lord Robert in a different light. He might not be an attractive proposition in himself, but if marriage to him finally brought recognition by Elizabeth of her rights to the English throne, then he was worth considering.

Pressing home the advantage, Elizabeth decided to make him even more acceptable, and in October 1564 she made him Earl of Leicester. It would have the added benefit of placating Robert himself. He had recently been showing signs of restiveness, fearing that Elizabeth might mean him really to marry Mary. That was the last thing he wanted. He had no desire to leave the English court. His place was there, at Elizabeth's side. When he heard that he was to be made Earl of Leicester at last, he did not know whether to be delighted or apprehensive. Indeed, his nervousness showed so plainly on his face as he knelt before the Queen during his investiture that she leaned forward with a smile and tickled him on the neck.

The French and Scottish ambassadors were standing close by, and they stared in disapproval at this unsuitable familiarity. Elizabeth then turned to Sir James Melville, the Scot, and asked him how he liked the new Earl. He made some suitable reply, whereupon she gave him a sidelong look and remarked, 'Yet you like better of yonder long lad', and she pointed across the room at Lord Darnley.

To please his mother, she had let the boy come to court and she allowed him to do a number of useful tasks, such as showing visiting dignitaries to her Presence Chamber. That day he had carried the sword of state before her in her procession. Sir James stiffened. Had she heard that he himself was involved in secret dealing with Lady Lennox? He replied quickly, 'No woman of spirit would make choice of such a man, for he was very lusty, beardless

85. King's College, Cambridge, visited by Elizabeth in 1564.
(Photograph, A F Kersting)

and lady-faced', then stood wondering what she had really meant. Was she about to propose a new candidate for his Queen's hand?

She was indeed. Perhaps because Robert was obviously on the verge of refusing to go on playing his part in the charade, perhaps because Mary herself was taking the plan too seriously, Elizabeth had decided that it was time to put an end to this particular diversion. Another harmless suitor was needed instead, and who better than young Lord Darnley? She had watched him in recent weeks and she could see that there was nothing in him. His mother was always telling her how obedient and respectful he was. It would be safe enough to send him north. Mary would take an interest in him because of his Tudor blood, and then Elizabeth could recall him to her court whenever she wished. He was her subject, for he had been born in England, and he owed his allegiance to her.

Having given this first hint of her new plan, Elizabeth turned her attention to the Scottish ambassador. Melville was shrewd, she could see that. He could be a useful source of information. Rather to his discomfiture, she summoned him sometimes as many as three times a day. They discussed Anglo-Scottish relations, of course, and during one conversation she made her usual remark about being resolved to live and die a virgin – unless, of course, Mary ignored all her advice and forced her into matrimony. 'Madam', he replied, 'You need not tell me that. I know your stately stomach. You think, if you were married, you would be but Queen of England; and now you are King and Queen both. You may not endure a commander'. He was more accurate in his assessment of her than many historians have been since.

Aware that he would carry stories about her back to Edinburgh as well as revealing useful details about Mary, Elizabeth set out on a campaign to impress him. Each day, she wore a different outfit. One day it was in the English fashion, the next day her costume was French, and then Italian, and she did not hesitate to ask him which he thought suited her best. 'I said the Italian dress', Sir James recalled, years later, 'which pleased her well, for she delighted to show her golden coloured hair, wearing a caul [a close-fitting cap] and bonnet as they do in Italy. Her hair was more reddish than yellow, curled in appearance naturally. Then she entered to discern what colour of hair was reputed best, and whether my Queen's hair or hers was the best, and which of them two was fairest.'

It was all rather embarrassing, and Sir James tried to evade the question. 'I answered that the fairness of them both was not their worst fault', but she persisted. Trying again, he said that she was the fairest queen in England and Mary was the fairest queen in Scotland. Even then Elizabeth was not satisfied until he finally declared that 'they were both the fairest ladies of their courts and that Her Majesty was whiter, but our Queen was very lovely'.

She digested that in silence for a moment, and then out came another question. 'She enquired which of them was of highest stature. I said, our Queen. Then, saith she, she is too high, and that herself was neither too high nor too low. Then she asked what kind of exercises she used. I answered that [when] I was dispatched out of Scotland the Queen was lately come from the Highland hunting; that when she had leisure from the affairs of her country, she read upon good books, the histories of diverse countries, and sometimes would play upon the lute and virginals. She asked if she played well. I said, reasonably for a queen.'

Nothing more was said, but that very day after dinner, Elizabeth sent her cousin Lord Hunsdon to fetch Sir James to a quiet gallery in her palace. Hunsdon was not supposed to say why, but he warned the ambassador that he was about to hear the Queen perform on the virginal. Sure enough, the

86. *Henry Carey, Lord Hunsdon*, by an unknown artist.
(By kind permission of the Trustees of the Will of the 8th Earl of Berkeley: photograph, Courtauld Institute of Art)

85

87. *Henry, Lord Darnley*, painted by an unknown artist about the time he went to Scotland.
(Scottish National Portrait Gallery)

sound of music came from Elizabeth's chamber as they approached. Cautiously, Sir James pushed aside the tapestry in front of the door and crept in, to stand silently listening. After a moment or two Elizabeth appeared to notice him for the first time. She stopped abruptly and came forward, 'seeming to strike me with her left hand and alleging that she used not to play before men, but when she was solitary, to shun melancholy'.

When she enquired how he came to be there, he said smoothly, 'As I was walking with my Lord of Hunsdon, as we passed by the chamber-door, I heard such melody as ravished me and drew me within the chamber, I knew not how'. Delighted with this courtly response, Elizabeth sat down on a cushion and when he knelt beside her 'she gave me a cushion with her own hand, to lay under my knee, which at first I refused, but she compelled me to take it'.

The usual interrogation then began. Who played better, herself or Mary? When he had produced an acceptable answer to that, she quizzed him about his own linguistic abilities and his tastes in reading, then she insisted that he stay in London for two more days, until he could see her dance: 'Which being done, she enquired of me whether she or my Queen danced best. I answered that the Queen danced not so high and disposedly as she did . . .'

After an encounter with Lord Robert, who declared himself not worthy to wipe the shoes of the Queen of Scots and tried to blame the entire courtship on 'his secret enemy' William Cecil, Sir James was finally allowed to take his leave. As he made his farewells, Cecil placed a fair chain about his neck, and Lady Lennox gave him presents to deliver in Scotland, including a diamond ring for Mary, a diamond for Lord James, and a diamond and ruby watch for Maitland of Lethington, 'for she was still in good hope that her son, my Lord Darnley, would come better speed than the Earl of Leicester concerning the marriage of our Queen', Melville noted.

A few months later, in February 1565 Lord Darnley set off for Scotland. Elizabeth had finally allowed him to go north to join his father. She had done so against the advice of Cecil. He had been warning her interminably of the dangers of uniting the two claims to the English throne, but she refused to listen. She was confident that the lad would do whatever she told him.

According to the reports that came back, Mary greeted him politely enough but she did not seem interested in him. Elizabeth therefore announced that even if Mary did marry Leicester, she could not recognise her as heir to the English throne.

That had the desired effect. Mary's only reason for marrying the Earl had been removed, and once Elizabeth's envoy had gone, she wept bitterly. The English Queen had made a fool of her, she said, luring her on with false promises, and in her frustration and rage she turned to Darnley. Hitherto she had been willing to marry with Elizabeth's advice, she said. Now she would make her own choice. Her cousin Henry was tall and handsome. Lady Lennox was always writing to extol his virtues. Mary began to spend hours in his company and when he fell ill with measles she nursed him and thought herself in love with him.

Reading her ambassador's dispatches, Elizabeth grew alarmed. This affair, intended as a passing diversion for Mary, was becoming far too serious. Cecil was assuring her that Mary really would marry Darnley, and so she ordered her own Privy Council to sign a declaration warning that Mary would jeopardise their friendship if she went ahead. She instructed her ambassador to remonstrate with the Queen of Scots and she even reverted to the Leicester idea and said that she could only recognise Mary as heir if she married him, and no one else.

On 2 July 1565, she recalled both Darnley and his father to the English court. As her subjects, they ought to have obeyed her at once. Instead, they ignored her orders, and at the beginning of August she received the news she had been dreading. Mary had married Lady Lennox's son on 29 July 1565 at her Palace of Holyrood. He was now Henry, King of Scots. Elizabeth promptly sent the Countess back to the Tower of London once more.

Scotland was in such an unstable state that it was really impossible to predict what would happen next. When the disgruntled Lord James, now Earl of Moray, rebelled against his sister, Cecil was eager to help him, and not merely because they were fellow-Protestants. He had long since decided that the best way to keep England safe was, as he put it, to fan the fires in his neighbour's houses. Convincing Elizabeth to cooperate with a subject who was plainly defying his rightful monarch was a more difficult matter.

Cecil did manage to persuade Elizabeth to send Moray some money, but it did little good. Mary took the field against the rebels and soon they were fleeing south, confident that the Queen of England would help them. Reluctantly, Elizabeth agreed that Moray could come to her court. When he arrived, she and Cecil saw him secretly, to work out their plan of action. She did not want to offend the French by appearing too anxious to assist the rebels and so a careful little scene was devised.

When she received Moray and his friends the following day they knelt before her and begged for her assistance. She answered curtly that they had rebelled against their rightful monarch. They were lucky she was not going to throw them into prison. As it was, they were not to stay in England, but she and her Privy Council would intercede with Mary on their behalf. She then turned a blind eye to their continued presence in her kingdom.

Without Moray to guide her, Mary, Queen of Scots was finding it increasingly difficult to control her turbulent nobility, and all the more so because she had soon found out that her husband was not the handsome, reliable, obliging young man she had thought him. Weak, drunken, vain and immature, he was completely unsuited to his role as consort. His enemies were determined to remove him, and so they ensnared him in a complicated plot.

Mary was pregnant that winter. Exploiting the recent quarrels between her and her husband, they convinced him, quite unjustifiably, that the child was not his. His wife had been having an affair with her Italian secretary, David Riccio, they alleged, and they drew him into a scheme to murder the man, in Mary's own presence. Cecil and Elizabeth's ambassador in Edinburgh both knew the details of the murder plan days before Darnley and his friends burst into Mary's supper chamber and stabbed Riccio to death, but they probably kept it from Elizabeth lest she try to warn her sister-Queen. She was certainly affronted when she heard the news. When the Spanish ambassador visited her a few weeks later he found her ostentatiously wearing a gold miniature of Mary on a long chain, and she harangued him for more than an hour about the shocking events in Edinburgh. If she had been Mary, she said, she would have snatched Darnley's dagger from him and stabbed him to death.

Mary had not done that, but she had been resourceful. She had escaped from the immediate danger and she had not, as her adversaries had calculated, arrested her husband for murder. Instead, she effected an uneasy reconciliation with him and their son, the future James VI and I, was born safely on 19 June 1566. Four days later, Sir James Melville arrived in London with the news.

It was a Sunday, and he found Elizabeth dancing merrily after supper. According to his account, he told Cecil, who went across and whispered something to the Queen. Immediately, she sat down, rested her cheek on her hand and remained silent for a few moments, and then she exclaimed 'that the Queen of Scotland was lighter of a fair son, and that she was but a barren stock'. She soon recovered her equanimity, however. This baby was a very important infant. One day, he might unite the kingdoms of England and Scotland. She recognised that, even if her own subjects were not willing to admit it. With uncharacterstic generosity, she sent north a huge enamelled gold font set with precious stones, and she agreed to be his godmother.

88. *James Douglas, 4th Earl of Morton,* one of the murderers of Riccio, painted in 1577 by an unknown artist.
(Scottish National Portrait Gallery)

7

THE DUKE OF NORFOLK

THREE MONTHS later, even more dramatic news arrived from the north. Lord Darnley was dead, killed after an explosion which demolished the house near Edinburgh where he had been staying. His body had been found in the garden, beneath a tree. He had either been strangled or asphyxiated. The Earl of Bothwell was generally believed to be the murderer, and everyone was saying that he was Mary's lover.

Elizabeth was appalled. A fortnight after the murder took place, she wrote Mary a letter, in French. 'My ears have been so astounded and my heart so frightened to hear of the horrible and abominable murder of your husband and my own cousin', she began, 'that I have scarcely spirit to write: yet I cannot conceal that I grieve more for you than him.' Reports suggested that Mary was not going to take any action against the murderers. If she failed to prosecute them, said Elizabeth, she would be ruined, for everyone would say that she was a party to the crime. 'I should not do the office of a faithful cousin and friend', Elizabeth went on, 'if I did not urge you to preserve your honour, rather than look through your fingers at revenge on those who have done you that pleasure, as most people say. I counsel you so to take this matter to heart that you show the world what a noble Princess and loyal woman you are. I write thus vehemently, not that I doubt, but for affection . . .'

Elizabeth had confronted a very similar situation herself when Leicester was suspected of murdering Amy Robsart. She had realised how fatal it would be to her reputation, to her very future, if she married him, and that was why she had banished him from her court and given up any thought of taking him as a husband. In warning Mary to follow a similar course she was perfectly

89. Drawing of the scene at Kirk o' Field after the murder of Lord Darnley. He lies dead beneath a tree, his servant's body nearby.
(Public Record Office, London)

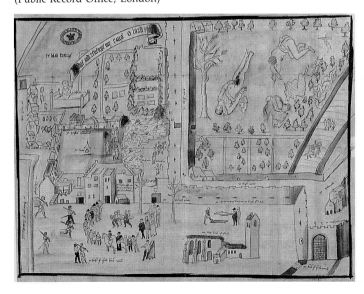

90. *James Hepburn, 4th Earl of Bothwell,*
third husband of Mary, Queen of Scots:
miniature by an unknown artist.
(Scottish National Portrait Gallery)

sincere, and indeed Mary's own friends and relatives on the continent were urgently pressing upon her that same advice; but she would not listen and in May she became Bothwell's wife.

When Elizabeth heard about the wedding, her response was blunt and to the point. 'No good friend you have in the whole world can like thereof', she told Mary, 'and if we should otherwise write or say, we should abuse you. For how could a worse choice be made for your honour than in such haste to marry such a subject who, besides other notorious lacks, public fame has charged with the murder of your late husband . . .'

As everyone had predicted, ruin swiftly followed Mary's third marriage. Two months after the wedding her subjects rose up against her and imprisoned her in the island Castle of Lochleven, while her husband fled to Scandinavia. Cecil and the other English statesmen might be relieved that the woman they considered to be their own Queen's arch-enemy was safely under lock and key, but Elizabeth herself could only feel outrage that a fellow-monarch was being treated in this manner by her subjects. It was a shocking precedent, and something would have to be done to remedy matters at once.

She decided to dispatch a special envoy to remonstrate with the Scottish Protestant leaders, and she chose Sir Nicholas Throckmorton. He was to ride north immediately and seek out the rebels. 'What warrant have they, in Scripture, as subjects, to depose their Prince?' she demanded angrily, and she told him, 'Plainly denounce them that if they determine the deprivation of the Queen their sovereign lady of her royal estate, we are determined . . . that we will take plain part against them to revenge their sovereign, for an example to all posterity . . .'

She did not wish to appear to be condoning Mary's actions, of course, and so he was to assure the lords that 'we do detest and abhor the murder committed upon our cousin their King and mislike as much as any of them the marriage of the Queen our sister with Bothwell. But herein we dissent from them, that we think it not lawful nor tolerable for them, being by God's ordinance subjects, to call her, whom also by God's ordinance is their superior and Prince, to answer to their accusations by way of force, for we do not think it consonant in nature the head should be subject to the foot'.

She was in a rage about it for days and, ignoring her own anxious Privy Councillors, she declared that she would make war against the Scots. Cecil was horrified. That could lead to incalculable disasters, he said, and he pleaded with her not to contemplate such a drastic course. She paid no heed to his arguments, and she was only persuaded not to take military action when he

91. *Sir Nicholas Throckmorton*, relative of Katherine Parr, and Elizabeth's envoy to Scotland, painted by an unknown French artist about 1562. (National Portrait Gallery, London)

convinced her that if she sent an army north Mary would be killed by her captors. Muttering that she would try economic sanctions instead, she gave up her more bloodthirsty threats and Cecil breathed a sigh of relief.

In fact, her envoy's intervention had already saved Mary's life. The Scottish lords had been insisting that their Queen must abdicate and Throckmorton was alarmed to hear that she was refusing to do so. He was convinced that they would kill her if she continued to defy them. He failed in his attempts to get to Lochleven to see her, but he did manage to smuggle a message to her, urging her to give in and sign the abdication papers to save her life. She could easily disavow them afterwards, for any such documents extorted by force would be illegal.

In the end, she followed his advice. She had been pregnant when they took

92. *The Memorial of Lord Darnley*, painted in London by Livinus de Vogelaare for the Earl and Countess of Lennox, demanding vengeance for their son's death. They kneel by his tomb with their younger son, Charles.
(Reproduced by gracious permission of Her Majesty The Queen)

93. The Lennox Jewel, made for the Countess of Lennox in the 1570s, with complex emblems and inscriptions expressing the hope that her grandson James VI of Scotland will inherit the English throne.
(Reproduced by gracious permission of Her Majesty The Queen)

her to Lochleven. Now she miscarried of twins and as she lay in bed, weak from loss of blood, Lord Ruthven brutally threatened her with death if she would not abdicate. Declaring over and over again that she was acting under duress, she scrawled her name on his papers. Five days later, her little son was crowned King and the Earl of Moray became Regent of Scotland on his return from exile. Elizabeth refused to acknowledge his new position, but no doubt she was relieved that this experienced ally was in charge once more. As he himself said to Cecil, 'Although the Queen's Majesty your mistress outwardly seems not altogether to allow the present state here, yet doubt I not but her Highness in her heart likes it well enough'.

The uneasy peace was shattered the following spring when startling news arrived at the English court. Mary had escaped from her prison and had raised an army, only to be defeated at the Battle of Langside. Fleeing south, she had now crossed the River Solway into England. She was being held at Carlisle Castle and she was demanding permission to see the Queen of England in person so that she could ask for assistance.

Elizabeth's immediate reaction was that she must do something to help her beleaguered fellow-sovereign. Calling an emergency meeting of her Privy Council, which she herself attended, she spoke passionately on Mary's behalf. This rightful monarch, chosen by God to reign over Scotland, had been unlawfully deposed and ejected from her kingdom by her rebellious subjects. She must be restored at once. A heated debate ensued. Risking her wrath, Cecil and his colleagues spoke urgently against the idea. Mary was not an abused innocent, they said. She was Elizabeth's personal enemy, the woman who for years had been plotting to oust her and usurp the English throne. She must be handed over to the Scots so that Lord Moray could go on governing that country in the Protestant interest.

Elizabeth refused to contemplate that. In the present turmoil, they would be sending Mary to her death. If they did not hand her over, however, what was to be done with her? They did not want her in England, attracting the support of the Roman Catholics, nor could she be allowed to seek help in France. In the end, they reached an uneasy compromise. Mary would be held

94. Bolton Castle, North Yorkshire, where Mary, Queen of Scots
was held after her flight south.
(Photograph, A F Kersting)

in the north of England until a public enquiry could be set up to investigate
her part in Lord Darnley's murder. Once all the evidence had been heard,
Elizabeth would decide her fate. Even as they agreed this, Cecil and the other
councillors had the sinking feeling that their Queen had already made up her
mind about what she would do. Whatever the enquiry discovered, she seemed
determined to restore the Queen of Scots.

The proceedings opened on 4 October 1568. Mary was not allowed to attend,
nor did Elizabeth take part. She did not wish to be too closely associated with
the investigation, and so she insisted that it should be held as far from
London as was practicable. York was chosen as a suitable place and there the

95. The casket in which, it
was claimed, the
incriminating letters from
Mary, Queen of Scots to the
Earl of Bothwell were found.
(The Duke of Hamilton, at
Lennoxlove)

93

participants gathered: the Earl of Moray with his friends and advisers, the Bishop of Ross accompanied by Mary's other commissioners, and Elizabeth's own representatives, led by her kinsman Thomas, Duke of Norfolk.

The enquiry began with Mary's commissioners putting her complaints against her subjects, and then Moray read out his counter-charges. He did not accuse his half-sister outright of murdering Darnley, but he complained that she had failed to prosecute Bothwell for the crime. He also let it be known that he had in his possession a casket full of incriminating letters from Mary to Bothwell, proving that she had been his accomplice and had actually lured Darnley to his death.

The letters have long since disappeared, but modern scholars are agreed that that were not authentic. They had probably been concocted by some of Moray's people, for they are full of inconsistencies and irrelevancies. Significantly, he refused to produce them in public, although they were shown to the Duke of Norfolk, who expressed his horrified disapproval and sent a summary of the contents to Elizabeth.

She may or may not have believed them to be genuine. Her reaction has gone unrecorded, but in any event she was probably not too concerned about their status. She was not sitting in judgment on Mary's innocence or guilt. Ever a realist, she knew perfectly well that monarchs were often driven into less than Christian acts in order to safeguard their position. She wanted the enquiry to exonerate Mary, partly if not entirely, so that she could be allowed to rule jointly with Moray. That would keep her safely out of the way, and it would satisfy the French, who were agitating for her to help the royal fugitive. Mary was, after all, the sister-in-law of the French king.

Unfortunately for this scheme, events were not going according to plan. Mary's enemies were building up a convincing case against her and if they were allowed to continue, Elizabeth would be unable to achieve her preferred solution. To make matters worse, there were disquieting rumours about her chief commissioner's behaviour. The Duke of Norfolk, a thin-faced, dark-haired young man in his early thirties had been widowed three times and he was once more single, and extremely eligible. A few days after the enquiry opened, Maitland of Lethington invited him to go out hawking. They had met before, in the weeks preceding the Treaty of Edinburgh, and as they rode along together in companionable conversation, Maitland began to tell the Duke about his exciting new scheme.

Like Cecil, Maitland was a devious and expert politician. His motives were often impenetrable, but his overriding aim was to achieve the union of Scotland and England and for this purpose he wanted Mary back on the Scottish throne. Looking meaningfully at Norfolk, he said that if she were to marry a trustworthy, reliable Englishman of high rank, her husband could keep her in order and they could rule Scotland together. Who better to assume this role than the Duke?

At first Norfolk was astonished and alarmed. Elizabeth would never allow it . . . or would she? Maitland soon convinced him that he would be doing her a great favour if he lent himself to the notion. With startling rapidity, Cecil's spies got wind of the conspiracy and he warned Elizabeth that she could not trust her chief commissioner. The whole affair was getting out of hand, and she announced abruptly that she was transferring the enquiry to London.

On 25 November the hearing resumed in the Painted Chamber at Westminster before a new English commission which included Sir William Cecil and the Earl of Leicester. This time Moray openly accused his half-sister of procuring the murder of Darnley and produced the casket with its letters. There was a strong feeling in England now that Mary was guilty, and so Elizabeth could not risk finding in her favour.

On 10 January, Cecil read out a document stating that neither Mary's complaints against her subjects nor theirs against her had been proved. Moray was allowed to return to Scotland, with a loan of £5000, but Mary was sent to the grim castle at Tutbury, to be held in closer confinement. Once the hostility against her had faded, Elizabeth would try to restore her, on condition that she ratify the Treaty of Edinburgh, that Moray continue as Regent and young James VI be sent to London as a hostage for his mother's good behaviour. Elizabeth and Cecil believed that they had foreseen all eventualities, but they had reckoned without the unpredictable behaviour of the Duke of Norfolk. In the spring of 1569 he entered into correspondence with Mary, Queen of Scots. Their marriage plan had been revived.

At first Mary was cautious. She refused to involve herself, saying she could not consider the match unless Elizabeth agreed. She was told that Elizabeth approved and, desperate for some means of escape from her imprisonment, she hoped to divorce Bothwell and marry Norfolk instead. By early summer she and the Duke were exchanging love tokens, and by autumn Elizabeth was sure that something was amiss. She was not suspicious of Norfolk only. He would never have the imagination or the daring to initiate such a scheme, she felt sure. Others must be behind it and she very much feared that some of her lords had a sinister purpose in mind. They wanted to depose her in favour of Mary and her fourth husband.

She tried to extract the details from the Scots, for Moray seemed to know what was going on, but he was irritatingly vague. He denied that the idea had been his and said merely that he had known about it. Elizabeth then turned to Norfolk himself. One day as she strolled in the gardens of Richmond Palace she saw him standing talking with friends. He had just arrived from London, she knew, and she beckoned him over.

He joined her, looking nervous. What news did he have to tell her, she asked. Nothing, he stammered, he knew of nothing. 'No!' exclaimed Elizabeth sarcastically. 'You come from London and can tell me no news of a marriage?' As he floundered about, trying to think of a reply, Lady Clinton happened to come up, the Queen's attention was distracted for a moment, and the Duke slipped away.

A fortnight later, she tried again. She invited him to dine with her in private, but although he chattered on about all manner of things he fell suddenly silent when she approached the subject of the marriage. Exasperated, she gave him a sharp nip, 'bidding him take heed to his pillow', in other words, warning him to take care whom he married. Even then he did not have the courage to confess. He was still deluding himself that she really knew all about it and approved.

Finally, it was the Earl of Leicester who revealed all the details to her. His dealings with Norfolk had been distinctly murky, and now he was determined to keep himself right whatever happened. Predictably, Elizabeth was furious and she told the Duke plainly that he must have no more treasonable correspondence with the Queen of Scots. Surely this time he would heed her warning and dissociate himself from the conspirators.

That proved impossible. His sister Jane was married to the Earl of Westmorland and she had urged her husband to join the Earl of Northumberland and other discontented Roman Catholics in armed rebellion. Realising the danger this would bring him, the Duke panicked and fled to his house of Kenninghall, in Norfolk. Elizabeth thought this must be the signal for the rebellion to begin. She immediately summoned him to court, gave orders for Mary to be held under much stricter surveillance in case the rebels tried to rescue her and arrested various other high-born suspects.

When Norfolk received her message he said that he could not come to court yet. He had just taken purgatives and he dared not venture out of doors. Ill or not, thundered Elizabeth, he must come at once, even if he had to make the journey in a litter. He submitted at once, and as soon as he arrived she sent him to the Tower. She was in such a rage that she wanted to prosecute him for treason, but Cecil assured her that she would find this impossible. The Duke had done nothing treasonable himself.

Furiously, she then turned her attention to Westmorland and Northumberland, ordering them south. They refused to come. Urged on by Lady Westmorland, they raised their rebellion and five days later they were marching into Durham with their forces. Elizabeth sent the Earl of Sussex north with an

96. *Thomas Howard, 4th Duke of Norfolk,* Elizabeth's kinsman and suitor of Mary, Queen of Scots, probably painted by Eworth.
(Reproduced by permission of His Grace the Duke of Norfolk)

97. Kenninghall, much altered since the time of the 4th Duke of
Norfolk, but the windows of this present building come from the
house he knew.
(Reproduced by permission of His Grace the Duke of Norfolk)

army and soon the earls were fleeing for safety to Scotland. Cecil was adamant
that the rebels must be dealt with severely, and in the aftermath of the revolt,
more than 700 men and women who had taken part were hanged for treason.

As always, Elizabeth was not concerned with the theological aspects of the
rebellion. It was her opinion that the rebels must be punished because they
had challenged royal authority, not because they wanted to restore the Mass.
Her sister had persecuted from religious conviction. She did not. In private
life, she tolerated and indeed befriended a number of Roman Catholics because
she valued them for other reasons. There was the Lincoln Cathedral organist
William Byrd, for instance, who became a Gentleman of the Chapel Royal the
following February. A composer of astonishing versatility, he wrote both

98. *Thomas Percy, 7th Earl of Northumberland,*
one of the leaders of the Northern Rising,
by George Gower.
(National Trust, at Petworth)

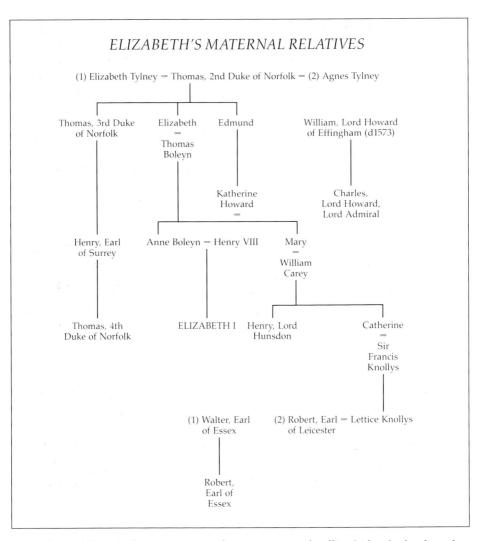

ELIZABETH'S MATERNAL RELATIVES

(1) Elizabeth Tylney = Thomas, 2nd Duke of Norfolk = (2) Agnes Tylney

Thomas, 3rd Duke of Norfolk

Elizabeth = Thomas Boleyn

Edmund

William, Lord Howard of Effingham (d1573)

Katherine Howard =

Charles, Lord Howard, Lord Admiral

Henry, Earl of Surrey

Anne Boleyn = Henry VIII

Mary = William Carey

Thomas, 4th Duke of Norfolk

ELIZABETH I

Henry, Lord Hunsdon

Catherine = Sir Francis Knollys

(1) Walter, Earl of Essex

(2) Robert, Earl = Lettice Knollys of Leicester

Robert, Earl of Essex

secular and liturgical music ranging from pavans and galliards for the keyboard to masses, anthems, motets and madrigals. In 1575 he and his former master Thomas Tallis obtained a patent from the Queen giving them the monopoly of selling sheet-music in England, and she allowed them to dedicate a volume of sacred songs to her.

This was in spite of the fact that Byrd's Catholicism was widely known. He was often to be found in the houses of the Roman Catholic nobility and during the subsequent years of persecution he composed a series of Latin motets with hidden meanings. The lament for Jerusalem, for example, plainly echoed the plight of those of his own faith under a Protestant monarch. Even so, Elizabeth continued to employ him, apparently extending her protection to him and his family. Whatever his religious affiliations, he was personally loyal to her, and his beautiful music soothed her after long hours of wrestling with her political problems.

The rising in the north had been a worrying disturbance of the domestic peace, but the most significant aspect of the whole affair was that the rebels had received promises of Spanish help. The Duke of Alva, Philip II's Governor of the Netherlands, had already sent Mary, Queen of Scots 10,000 ducats although he had foreseen that the rebellion would collapse and he feared that it would do her more harm than good. Philip himself always took so long to make up his mind about anything that it was all over before he came to a decision, but his hostility towards Elizabeth was now plain for all to see.

There was an added complication, too, when Pope Pius V issued a declaratory sentence against 'Elizabeth, Pretender Queen of England', deposing her and absolving all her subjects from their oath of allegiance to her. Henceforth, anyone who obeyed her orders would be excommunicated. The Pope had been under the misapprehension that the Northern Rising had succeeded when he issued his sentence, but whatever the circumstances it could have been extremely damaging, and Elizabeth made sure that it was not published in England.

That summer, the Duke of Norfolk, still in the Tower, made a humble submission to Elizabeth and, sure that he would cause no trouble, she released him. Her judgment of character was faulty on this occasion, for within a matter of weeks he had become embroiled in a new plot. Robert Ridolfi, an Italian banker living in England, had resolved to revive the plan to replace Elizabeth with Mary and Norfolk, the Duke of Alva again agreed to help, and Mary herself gave her approval to the scheme. Unfortunately for the Duke, Cecil's espionage network soon found evidence that he was corresponding with Ridolfi, who had by now left the country, and in August Norfolk was

99. William Byrd's anthem, 'O Lord, Make Thy Servant Elizabeth to rejoice in Thy Strength'.
(The Governing Body of Christ Church, Oxford: manuscript Mus.MS.988, wrongly numbered 58 for 57)

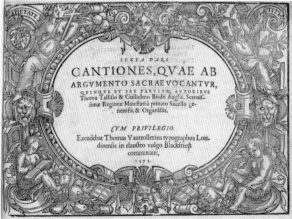

100. Title page of the sixth part of the *Cantiones*, dedicated by Thomas Tallis and William Byrd to Elizabeth, 1575.
(The British Library)

101. *Elizabeth I and the Three Goddesses*, by Eworth, 1569, showing Juno, Pallas and Venus retiring in confusion before the Queen's beauty and accomplishments.
(Reproduced by gracious permission of Her Majesty The Queen)

caught sending money and messages to the Bishop of Ross and some of Mary's other supporters. When the Bishop was arrested and interrogated, he confessed everything: Norfolk was sent back to the Tower, and Charles IX of France decided to stop trying to intervene on Mary's behalf and leave her to her fate. 'Alas', he sighed, 'the poor fool will never cease until she loses her head.'

102. *James VI of Scotland* as a child, by Arnould van Brounckhorst.
(Scottish National Portrait Gallery)

100

103. *Elizabeth I* in 1572, at the age of thirty-eight, Hilliard's earliest miniature of her. (National Portrait Gallery, London)

In January 1572 Elizabeth at last recognised James VI as King of Scots and that same month the Duke of Norfolk was brought before the peers in Westminster Hall, found guilty of high treason and sentenced to death. Throughout the spring he remained in the Tower, protesting his innocence of any evil intention against the Queen, while she agonised over the signing of his death warrant. Her anger had passed and she could not bring herself to end the life of this quiet, amiable young relative whom she had always

104. Rye, visited by Elizabeth in 1573: a view of Mermaid Street. (Photograph, A F Kersting)

liked. Cecil and the other Privy Councillors fumed over the delay. 'The Queen's Majesty hath been always a merciful lady, and by mercy she hath taken more harm than by justice', Cecil complained. Everyone knew that traitors must die, and for her own safety she must accept that. Three times she signed the death warrant, and three times she revoked it at the last minute.

In March, she was seriously ill with gastroenteritis and her councillors feared for her life. She had merely eaten bad fish, she said tersely when she began to recover, but her ministers had once more been forced to confront the prospect of her dying without an heir, and they were determined that she should summon parliament. She knew that they would try to force her to execute the Queen of Scots as well as the Duke, but she had to agree to let parliament meet, and the members duly assembled in May.

A special committee of both houses was appointed to discuss the problem of Mary, Queen of Scots and its members were blunt in their demands. Elizabeth must 'cut off her head and make no more ado about her', they said. She refused. 'Partly for honour, partly for conscience, partly for causes to herself known', she would not let them prosecute Mary for treason, or even rule her out of the succession. They drafted another bill ruling out of the succession anyone charged with trying to claim the English crown during Elizabeth's lifetime, but although she thanked them for their concern she said afterwards, 'We misliked it very much, being not of the mind to offer extremity or injury to any person'.

Her motives were not entirely altruistic. On 19 April 1572 her representatives had signed the Treaty of Blois with France agreeing that if either country were attacked, the other would come to its aid. She had found an ally at last, and she had no desire to jeopadise this valuable new relationship by executing the King of France's sister-in-law. She was aware, of course, that there was a price to be paid for her refusal to let parliament have its way. She declined to contemplate Mary's execution, but she could delay the Duke of Norfolk's death no longer. She signed the warrant, and he was beheaded at Tower Hill on 2 June.

The following month, Elizabeth set off on her usual summer progress. She liked to spend from mid-July until the end of September out of London, touring around her own castles and the houses of the aristocracy, enjoying the hunting when it was available. These excursions were famous, not least for the worry and expense they caused her hosts. They had to find food, drink and accommodation for the royal household, they had to provide the Queen herself with sumptuous apartments, they had to lay on suitable enter-tainments for her and they were expected to ply her with gifts, usually in the form of valuable jewellery.

Elizabeth looked forward to augmenting her collection of personal adorn-ments from such sources. One summer, she returned from her progress with a brooch in the form of a gold and crystal falcon set with rubies and emeralds, a phoenix and a salamander of agate, rubies and diamonds, a mother of pearl dolphin ridden by a gold and diamond man, a gold eagle set with diamonds and a gold maiden riding on a gold mermaid. The jewels were intricate, symbolic and enamelled in brilliant colours. A falcon was a favourite design, for it had been her mother's emblem, and the phoenix was one of her own.

Her progresses usually traversed the south-eastern counties of England, although she did once make a long and exciting visit to Bristol. Whichever direction she chose, she would spend from one to six nights at each house, according to its resources and her own whim. She was quite liable to cause havoc with all her steward's careful arrangements if she suddenly tired of a place or decided that the hospitality was not up to standard and gave orders to move on a day or two earlier than expected. In the summer of 1572 she called upon Cecil at Burghley House near Stamford and Sir Nicholas Bacon at his mansion of Gorhambury near St Albans, as well as including in her circuit the Earl of Bedford, Lord Compton and Lord Berkeley.

She was accompanied on her progresses by many of her courtiers, although they were continually seeking to excuse themselves so that they could spend a little time on their own estates. Not only the noblemen were affected, of course. All the local people along the way were drawn into the celebrations and for weeks beforehand they were busy rehearsing pageants, tidying up their villages and composing suitable speeches of welcome.

During her visit to Kent in the summer of 1573 she delighted the people of Rye by spending three days in their town before moving eastwards by way of Sissinghurst to Dover. She stayed for almost a week in Dover Castle, then she moved on to the thriving port of Sandwich. The mayor and his jurats were waiting on the edge of the town to welcome her, accompanied by 300 men in white doublets and black hose, a compliment to the Queen since these were her personal colours.

The streets were newly gravelled and they had been strewn with fresh rushes and herbs. Householders had decked their doorways with branches of greenery, and cords of vine branches were strung across the streets to support garlands of flowers. The minister of St Clement's Church made a speech and presented the Queen with a gold cup and a copy of the New Testament in Greek. She smiled as if she had never been given such presents before, and said that his speech had been 'both very well handled and very eloquent'. Her audience glowed with pleasure and her few words were eagerly memorised, repeated and recorded.

As she rode towards Mr Manwood's house, where her father had twice stayed, each post she passed had a sheet of paper attached to it, with a welcoming poem. There was a grand entertainment when a model fort was besieged and then they all sat down in the schoolhouse, at a table 28 feet long, for a grand banquet. It was the schoolmaster's turn to make a speech and to present her with a very striking covered cup in silver gilt, 'nearly a cubit high'. The Queen was very merry and even the heavy rain next morning did not spoil her appreciation of the sight of about a hundred English and Dutch children sitting spinning on a special platform in the schoolhouse yard. That afternoon, she and all her lords and ladies rode for Canterbury, leaving the townspeople half-dazed with exhaustion, excitement and the feeling that their lives had been touched briefly by something wonderful.

For Elizabeth, occasions such as these were not merely a relaxation. She always enjoyed seeing new places but, more than that, she knew that it was an extremely useful means of binding her subjects to her. She could never rely on the loyalty of her lords and so she was eager to cultivate the goodwill of her ordinary subjects. That did not mean that they could be familiar or outspoken. With her very hierarchical view of society she expected them to obey and to keep to their place. They would be punished if they were disobedient, but on golden September afternoons when they lined the streets to cheer her and fumbled their way through their carefully prepared orations, she listened to them with kindly patience and she appreciated to the full their reassuring flattery.

8

THE FRENCH SUITORS

BACK IN LONDON, Elizabeth resumed her accustomed routine, striding briskly through her gardens, pouring out a torrent of impromptu Latin at some visiting ambassador, interrupting a sermon with a caustic command to the preacher to stop talking nonsense and keep to the point. A creature of strong convictions in spite of her apparent vacillation, she disliked novelties and she had no patience with rambling discourses when there was business to be done. She herself had long since mastered the art of saying nothing in elaborate, incomprehensible terms, but when an envoy or an official went on too long with his carefully rehearsed oration she would cut him short with one of her sharp, deflating remarks.

She expected to be flattered, of course, and not just because of female vanity. William Cecil and the others had learned at the very start that they must address her in tones of grovelling humility, for that showed that they knew their place. She might be robust and jocular in her manner but any hint of opposition or over-familiarity and she was at her most imperious. She knew that she must constantly strive to keep these ambitious men in check, for given the slightest opportunity they would try to dominate her. She could, of course, manipulate them with promises of honours or high office. In 1571 Cecil was created Lord Burghley and he became Treasurer after that, but with her limited resources she could not offer such rewards frequently. Instead, she had to use other methods.

To this end, she developed and exaggerated many of the natural traits in her personality. She was quick-tempered, and when she was angry she allowed herself to bellow and shout. Not only did that cow her officials: it also earned their respect. She could see them looking at her with reluctant admiration and rather than resenting this treatment they told each other happily that she was just like her father.

105. Ring which opens to show portraits of both Elizabeth and her mother, Anne Boleyn, about 1575.
(Trustees of Chequers)

106. *Elizabeth I* in about 1575, perhaps by Federigo Zuccaro.
(National Portrait Gallery, London)

Again, she deliberately cultivated her feminine wilfulness. Because she was highly intelligent and she could see all the possibilities in any situation, she was often in a genuine dilemma as to which decision to take. However, while she probably knew quite well which course she would eventually choose, it suited her to play up her indecisiveness and her changeability. If her statesmen knew what she was going to do, they could take steps to counter her. She had enough trouble with them in that respect already. They were continually keeping reports from her, failing to obey her instructions and engaging in petty quarrels with each other which held up the execution of state business. As long as they did not know what to expect next, they could not get together and hatch plots against her policies. It was far better to keep them guessing.

This was also why she exploited her penchant for disconcerting remarks. In part, it was because she was easily bored, and nothing livened up a tedious audience so much as a sudden interjection which had her visitor stop in mid-sentence, gape at her, turn red in the face and stammeringly lose the thread of what he was saying. Even better, she had long since learned that in an unguarded moment people were liable to come out with some piece of infor-mation they had been trying to keep secret from her. Her apparently eccentric asides could serve a very useful purpose.

She herself tried to give nothing away by mistake, and she knew she did not dare show any sign of weakness in front of those thrusting, ambitious opportunists, her courtiers. If she seemed to be in anything less than complete command, they would start trying to tell her what to do. To this end, she usually ignored any illness as much as possible, and fortunately she had excellent health. She did suffer from headaches and in her forties she was troubled by an ulcer in her leg, but she always brushed aside solicitous enquiries with a sharp answer. On the few occasions when she was really ill, she convalesced rapidly and got back to normal as quickly as she could. With her love of exercise and the outdoor life she retained her thin, youthful figure and that, combined with her abundant nervous energy, made her seem younger than she really was.

She had no desire for her subjects to think that she was getting older and losing her grip, so she did her best to preserve her youthful appearance. She always made a point of dressing magnificently, of course. All monarchs did. Their clothing was a visible sign of their majesty. Elizabeth's favourite colours were still black, white and orange, along with regal purple, but her garments were no longer the simple if dramatic costumes she had chosen as a girl. Now, they were encrusted with jewels and complicated trimmings. Her silk and velvet dresses had stiffened bodices thick with gems, her padded sleeves were intricately slashed and pinked, and her wide skirts over farthingale petticoats were elaborately embroidered with flowers and fruit and caterpillars and worms.

This grandeur was complemented on public occasions by her magnificent jewels. The costly, symbolic brooches were pinned to her hair or to her fine lace ruff, large pearl drops were suspended from her ears, heavy ropes of pearls were hung round her neck and expensive bracelets and rings empha-sised her beautiful hands. Some of these treasures had been inherited from her father, many were gifts and some she had bought. When the Portuguese Pretender Don Antonio was forced to flee from his country she purchased some of his jewels, and after Mary, Queen of Scots was imprisoned by her lords she managed to outbid Catherine de Medici for Mary's fabulous black pearls.

No matter how young Elizabeth might seem, of course, she could not conceal the fact that she was nearing the end of her childbearing years. Even so, Cecil continued to pray that she would marry, the House of Commons urged her to do so whenever they met, suitors still sought her hand and she herself was perfectly willing to engage in the elaborate game of courtship, for her own political purposes. In 1570, she therefore entered into marriage negotiations with the French.

Catherine de Medici was still ruling both Charles IX and his kingdom. A plump, dark-haired Italian with large, hooded eyes and heavy features, she was best known abroad for her deviousness and for the way she browbeat her sons. Francis, the eldest, was dead now and Charles was nearly twenty, but he was a delicate young man and he had been completely unable to break free from his mother's domination. Next to him came Henry, Duke of Anjou, Catherine's favourite. Not everyone liked him, of course. He had a disturbing habit of attending court masquerades dressed in extremely elaborate women's clothes and wearing heavy make-up. When he was not engaged in this favourite pastime, he was closeted with his priests, for he was a very fervent Roman Catholic.

Finally, there was the youngest son, the Duke of Alençon, a scrawny, undersized, belligerent teenager. His father had unwisely insisted on baptising him Hercules. Catherine called him Francis. The boys were spoiled, spiteful, jealous of each other and increasingly rebellious. Keeping them in order was almost as difficult as ruling France, Catherine felt, but they would be useful pawns in her foreign policy.

The rapprochement of 1570 between England and France was something new, after their long years of enmity, and there had never been any love lost between Elizabeth and Catherine. Both astute, autocratic women, they had never hidden their contempt for each other. Now, however, they felt the need to stand together against the growing threat from Spain, and there would be other benefits from an alliance for mutual defence. Catherine would no longer be likely to meddle in Scotland, Elizabeth would have to stop sending grudging and intermittent help to the French Huguenots, and the English alliance would strengthen Catherine's hand against her own enemy the Duke of Guise. Elizabeth therefore let it be known that she was willing to receive a proposal of marriage from France; Catherine suggested the effeminate Henry, and Elizabeth expressed enthusiastic gratitude.

She had recently appointed a new ambassador to the French court, the ultra-Protestant Sir Francis Walsingham. He would stir up as much trouble there as he could. What did the Duke of Anjou look like, she asked him. He was sallow in the face and his legs were long and thin, said Walsingham gloomily, but he was well-proportioned otherwise, though 'what helps he has

107. *Hercules-Francis, Duke of Alençon,*
Elizabeth's suitor, by J Decourt.
(Bibliothèque Nationale, Paris)

108. *Henry, Duke of Anjou*, later Henry III of France, by an unknown German artist.
(Bibliothèque Nationale, Paris)

109. *Catherine de Medici*, a miniature attributed to Clouet.
(By courtesy of the Board of Trustees of the Victoria and Albert Museum)

to supply the defects of nature' Sir Francis did not know. He did not pass on the comments of the Venetian ambassador, who had told his Senate, 'He is completely dominated by voloptuousness, covered with perfumes and essences. He wears a double row of rings and pendants at his ears'. In any event, Elizabeth was more concerned about his age. Walsingham advised her not to worry, saying that the Duke already bore himself 'like a man'. 'Yet he will always be younger than me', sighed Elizabeth, paving the way for her ultimate rejection of him. 'So much the better for you', leered the Earl of Leicester, who was standing at her side.

The following April, Catherine sent her experienced ambassador Guido Cavalcanti to England with a formal proposal and a suitably flattering portrait of Anjou. His appearance seemed satisfactory enough, Elizabeth thought, but his religion was a problem. Catherine wanted him and his household to be allowed to worship openly as Roman Catholics, she wanted him to be crowned King of England the very day after the wedding and she was demanding that he should go on ruling as king when Elizabeth died.

When she heard of these conditions, Elizabeth demurred. She would have to consult parliament, she said. Henry would probably be allowed to rule jointly with her, and she might even let him be called king, but there was certainly no question of his governing England once she was gone. When he heard all that, Philip II's old friend the Count de Feria laughed cynically. 'She will no more marry Anjou than she will marry me', he said, and he was right.

In August, the French sent another envoy with a revised offer. Elizabeth remarked annoyingly that she did not see why Anjou could not worship in the Church of England like everyone else and joked that she would have the Book of Common Prayer translated into Latin for him if that would help. It did not. He had never liked the idea and he was furious when he heard what she had said. She was 'not only an old creature but had a sore leg' he burst out in public, causing a diplomatic incident. Catherine de Medici was forced to apologise to Elizabeth for his rudeness, but it was plain that the scheme had collapsed.

Elizabeth gave out that she was affronted that her suitor had withdrawn his proposal. However, the exposure of the Ridolfi Plot at the end of the year made her willing to revive the subject. The threat from the Spanish was even greater than she had imagined: their active participation in the plot had shown her that. She told Catherine that she might consider making concessions if Anjou was still interested. Catherine replied that he was not. She would never be able to persuade him to go to England, and although she did not say so, she already had a new plan for his future. She was hoping to have him elected King of Poland. However, she went on, she did have another son. Hercules-Francis, Duke of Alençon, was seventeen now and he did not share the intense religious convictions of his elder brother. In such matters, he was likely to be 'a much less scrupulous fellow'. Would he do instead?

110. Warwick Castle, where Elizabeth entertained Monsieur de la Mole.
(Photograph, A F Kersting)

111. The Great Hall of Warwick Castle, photographed some years ago when Elizabeth's coronation portrait (plate 1) still hung there.
(Photograph, A F Kersting)

Apart from the fact that Elizabeth was thirty-eight and old enough to be his mother, the Duke was rumoured to be a hunchbacked dwarf, drastically disfigured by smallpox. In the game of diplomacy, however, no prince was too hideous to be rejected out of hand and when in June 1572 French delegates arrived in England to ratify the Treaty of Blois and formally offer him as a suitor, Elizabeth was all gracious encouragement. She would, of course, like to see him for herself, she said. This would not yet be possible, Catherine replied, but she would send over one of her son's friends, Monsieur de la Mole, to do the preliminary wooing for him. De la Mole duly arrived, had secret meetings with the Queen, supped with her at Warwick Castle, sat through a performance by her on the spinet and admired a spectacular fireworks display before departing for home.

The project might be no further forward, but Elizabeth was extremely anxious to keep it going because trouble seemed to be looming again on the continent. In one of the intermittent truces in the French religious wars, Catherine was showing signs of meddling in the Netherlands. This federation of Roman Catholic and Protestant states was ruled by a Regent on behalf of Spain, and for some years past the Protestant Dutch had been in open rebellion against Philip II's representative. Religion was never Catherine's principal motive for doing anything, and rather than supporting the Roman Catholics who might have been seen as her natural allies, she decided to give assistance to the Protestants. If she sent an army to drive the Spaniards out, that would keep Philip busy and the Dutch would be so grateful she would surely be able to persuade them to make her son the Duke of Alençon Regent instead. That would secure his future once and for all, without any need to sacrifice him to England's impossible Queen.

When she heard of this plan, Elizabeth was mightily alarmed. She did not like the Dutch. They were ultra-Protestant. Worse still, they were republicans and republicans were anathema to her. However, she feared the proximity of Spanish forces even more, and she would dearly have liked to see them driven out: not, however, by France. A French army so close at hand was equally menacing. Alençon's attention would have to be diverted. He would have to be convinced that she really was serious about taking him for her husband and Catherine would have to be made to recognise that this was a much cheaper and less troublesome way of finding a satisfactory role for her precious son.

112. *Persecuted Protestants in the Netherlands* brought before the Spanish Governor, the Duke of Alva, painted by an unknown artist.
(In a private collection)

113. *Henry of Navarre*, son-in-law of
Catherine de Medici and leader of
the French Protestants,
by P Dumoutier.
(Bibliothèque Nationale, Paris)

114. *Charles IX* in adult life, by Clouet.
(Bibliothèque Nationale, Paris)

It was all very difficult for Elizabeth. Much of her own popularity at home rested upon the fact that her subjects saw her as a defender of Protestantism, and here she was cultivating the Roman Cathlic French. To make matters worse, although Catherine de Medici had always assumed a fairly neutral stance between her warring subjects, she now instigated a murderous attack on her Protestants. In pursuit of her policy of religious reconciliation, she had arranged the marriage of her daughter Marguerite to Henry of Navarre, one of the Huguenot leaders. Instead of ushering in a new era of peace, the wedding had disastrous consequences. The celebrations were not even over when trouble flared between the opposing factions; Catherine panicked, and on her orders more than 8000 Huguenots died in the Massacre of St Bartholomew's Eve.

Elizabeth was on her summer progress to Bristol when the news came, and she avoided receiving the French ambassador for as long as she could. When they all arrived at Woodstock, however, on their way back to London, she took him aside and asked him for an explanation of what had happened. Although her subjects were ablaze with indignation, her own protest was mild. She was far more anxious for reassurance that recent events had not altered Catherine's attitude towards their alliance.

Fortunately, the Duke of Alençon had not been involved in planning the massacre: he had actually spoken out against it, but his habit of opposing everything his family suggested was not usually an advantage. He was the typical rebellious adolescent, constantly flouting his mother's orders and squabbling with his brothers. Out of perversity as much as anything else, he struck up a friendship with his sister's husband, Henry of Navarre, and by March 1574 the pair were under arrest for plotting to murder Charles IX.

Elizabeth sent an envoy to intercede on her suitor's behalf, but Catherine had far too much on her mind to pay attention to him. Charles's health, always precarious, had deteriorated rapidly and on 30 May 1574 he died. His brother Anjou, hastily summoned from Poland, set off for home to become King Henry III while Alençon, in floods of tears, flung himself at his mother's feet and swore perpetual allegiance to her.

She knew how much reliance to place on that. She had allowed him and Henry of Navarre to come back to court, but she was keeping them under close surveillance and she was perpetually plagued by their attempts to escape. She would have been tempted to let him go away and marry the Queen of England were it not that she distrusted Elizabeth's motives. She was sure that Elizabeth was going to use him against France for her own purposes, and she even suspected her of trying to spirit the boy away to England.

She was constantly on the alert. One night, after she had gone to bed, a guard came to wake her with the news that her youngest son was not in his bedchamber. She was up in an instant, marching through the palace to search all the rooms for him, until she finally came upon him sitting innocently chatting to his sister in her apartments. Partly reassured, she retired to bed again, but later that same week, her worst fears were realised.

Alençon, or rather, the Duke of Anjou as he had now become, said that he wanted to go to visit a friend in another part of Paris and he nagged at his mother until she gave him permission. Off he went in his coach, dismounted at the friend's house, hurried in at the front door and out again at the back door. There another coach was waiting to spirit him away. He had escaped from his family's clutches at last. Contrary to Catherine's imaginings, Elizabeth had had nothing to do with the incident and when she heard about it, she told Catherine that she could never take him as a husband while France was in such a state of disorder.

While Anjou travelled about the continent, now negotiating with William of Orange, leader of the Dutch Protestants, now visiting his own brother Henry III to vow loyalty to him, Elizabeth argued with her Privy Council about helping the Huguenots and the Dutch. Cecil and Leicester were continually urging her to assist her fellow-Protestants but she was as reluctant as

115. *William of Orange,* leader of the Protestants in the Netherlands, by an unknown artist.
(The Duke of Atholl, at Blair Castle)

116. Norwich Cathedral, visited by Elizabeth in 1578.
(Photograph, A F Kersting)

ever. Sometimes she promised money, but then she would procrastinate, change her mind and then change it back again. She did not want to offend either Philip II or Henry III by aiding their rebels. Indeed, she retained her rooted aversion to anybody's rebels and she had no desire to help any who were in opposition to their rightful prince.

Finally, William of Orange tired of her unfulfilled promises. He gave up hoping that she would send him money and instead he invited Anjou to invade the Netherlands and become their governor. Catherine and Henry tried to prevent Anjou from undertaking what they now regarded as a dangerous and embarrassing adventure, but he ignored them and in August 1578 he signed a treaty with the Protestant Dutch. Elizabeth was in Norwich when the news came, visiting the cathedral, listening to the usual laudatory speeches and enjoying the various pageants which had been prepared to welcome her to England's second city. Her immediate public reaction was to send a message of friendship and support to Philip II, and in private she resolved to divert Anjou once more with invitations to renew his courtship.

Many of her ministers were angry at her revival of the scheme, and none more so than Leicester. For years he had held on, hoping against hope that she would finally decide to settle down and marry him. He knew her aversion to the whole idea of matrimony, but he had always been confident that if she took any husband it would be him. He had stood by while she flirted with one foreign suitor after another. He had pandered to her every whim, joined in her tedious, sometimes alarming stratagems, flattered her with pageants and valuable gifts, joked with her, hunted with her and attended to all manner of wearisome business which she could not be bothered seeing to herself.

113

For years he and Burghley had formed her inner council, and he did have considerable political influence, but he realised at last that the position of consort could never be his.

He had not shunned women completely, of course. There had been mistresses, and at least one illegitimate child. Recently, he had become very friendly with Lettice Knollys, a daughter of one of the Queen's cousins and very much the same physical type as Elizabeth herself. Lettice was thin, red-haired and vivacious. She was also married. Her husband, Walter, Earl of Essex, was in Ireland trying to quell a rebellion against the Queen, and he conveniently died there.

When Lettice discovered late in the summer of 1578 that she was pregnant, her own family insisted that Leicester marry her and the ceremony took place at Wanstead House on 21 September. Two days later, Elizabeth and the court arrived at Wanstead on their progress, but Leicester and his bride said nothing. There was no knowing what Elizabeth would do when she found out. She had sent men and women to the Tower for clandestine marriages, and this time, when her favourite was the miscreant, the consequences were too frightening to contemplate.

Leicester's secret was safe that winter. Elizabeth was taken up with arrival of another of Anjou's friends, and she suspected nothing. Jean de Simier was lively and charming and he had arrived with a suite of sixty gentlemen and a series of coffers stuffed full of precious jewels, gifts for the Queen and her courtiers. She liked him, she nicknamed him her Monkey but she remained coy about the marriage itself. Did Anjou want her merely because he hoped 'to be King – or for her mental and personal qualifications?' she wondered aloud. She really would have to see him in person before she could accept his proposal.

De Simier simply laughed and flirted with her all the more. It was a fine thing for an old woman like her to be thinking of marriage, she told the

117. *Walter, 1st Earl of Essex,* Earl-Marshal of Ireland and first husband of Lettice Knollys, by an unknown artist, 1572. (National Portrait Gallery, London)

Spanish ambassador, and her Privy Councillors gravely discussed the dangers
of childbirth for the first time at forty-five. Leicester was particularly loud in
his condemnation of the match, and so Simier retaliated. He had heard the
rumours and he had made it his business to have them confirmed. He told
Elizabeth that her dear friend had married Lettice.

Everyone waited nervously as the storm broke. Beside herself with rage,

115

120. *Lettice Knollys, Countess of Essex*, and wife of Robert, Earl of Leicester, attributed to Gower. (Reproduced by permission of the Marquess of Bath, Longleat House, Warminster, Wiltshire)

she ordered Leicester to the Tower, but his friends intervened. Even his sworn enemy, the Earl of Sussex, spoke up for him, saying that it would never do to send a man to prison for making a legal marriage. Reluctantly, Elizabeth withdrew the order and said he must remain under house arrest at Greenwich instead. Her courtiers were relieved. It was not as bad as they had expected. She was wounded, it was true, and she felt that she had been betrayed by the very person she had always trusted, but in the end she forgave him although she nurtured a violent dislike of Lettice.

Possibly as a way of showing them how little she cared, she flirted outrageously with Anjou when he finally did appear at her court that April. He was not nearly as ugly as people had said. His face was marked with the smallpox, it was true, but he was not a dwarf and now that he has passed through his turbulent adolescence he was quick-witted, humorous and charming. She liked him, she accepted his lavish compliments with smiling pleasure, she nicknamed him 'Frog' and she infuriated her courtiers by showing off disgracefully, leaping about in dances even more energetically than she had done in her youth, waving and smiling to him conspiratorially as he stood watching. Leicester was furious.

When Anjou left for Paris a fortnight later, she promptly sent draft marriage articles after him. He was delighted. If his mother and his brother would not help him with money for the Netherlands, he believed that Elizabeth would. 'If Your Majesty went to Poland to obtain that kingdom, why should not I go to England with a similar object?' he demanded, when Henry III tried to persuade him to have nothing more to do with Elizabeth. That, replied Henry stiffly, had been very different. He had been elected King of Poland. Elizabeth was merely using the Duke for her own purposes.

When Anjou did get back to England in August, the Queen seemed over-joyed. She presented him with a golden key which opened every door in her palace, and a jewelled arquebus. He gave her a diamond ring worth 5000 crowns. They had long, private discussions and when he left for France he gave her another diamond, shaped like a heart. 'Now the world will see whether I, as was pretended, have made you prisoner or whether you have not rather made me a prisoner and yours ever most obliged', sighed Elizabeth.

His family were more opposed to his dealings with her than ever, but he slipped away secretly to see her in the summer of 1581 and he was back in England that autumn. Their relationship seemed to be reaching a climax. She sent into his bedchamber every morning with a cup of broth for him and on the evening of Ascension Day a startling scene took place in the gallery at Whitehall. The pair of them appeared there together and Elizabeth told the French ambassador loudly, before the entire company, that she meant her marriage to go ahead. She then turned to Anjou, kissed him on the lips, drew a ring from her own finger and gave it to him as a token that they were betrothed.

The entire court was thrown into disarray. They had never expected her actually to come to the point and they hardly knew what to think. The very next morning, however, Elizabeth sent for the Duke. With many a sigh, she told him that, after lying awake all night, she had decided to sacrifice her own personal happiness and put her subjects' interests first. She could not marry him . . . at present . . . although she might change her mind. The whole busi-ness had been one of her elaborate masquerades, designed to keep the French, the Spaniards and everyone else guessing.

The Duke expressed grave sorrow and disappointment, but he had probably been her accomplice in the gallery scene, just as Leicester had been forced to play his part in the Mary, Queen of Scots charades. Anjou did become a nuisance, though, for instead of departing meekly home he showed no desire to leave. He did not want to go back to his family to seek their help and so he hung around at court, irritating everyone with his presence.

Leicester wanted to bribe him to go away but when he suggested giving him £200,000 Elizabeth was horrified at the thought of parting with so much money. She tried telling Anjou that they would always be friends, but when she added that he must think of her as a sister, he burst into such floods of tears that she had to lend him her handkerchief to dry his eyes. In the end, she was forced to give him £10,000 in cash, with the promise of more to follow once he was safely out of the country. She went as far as Canterbury to see him on his way and Leicester escorted him over to Holland, bearing a secret letter from Elizabeth to William of Orange in which she urged him to keep her rejected suitor there at all costs and never let him return to England. When she finally knew that he had gone, she retired to her chamber, so it was said, to dance with glee, and then she amused herself by penning a heartbroken lament, 'On Monsieur's Departure'.

She wrote to him from time to time after that. Confident that he would not return, she told him that she would give a million pounds to see her Frog swimming happily in the Thames once more. For his part, he never did succeed in making himself Governor of the Netherlands and two and a half years later he died of a fever. Elizabeth put her court into mourning. He had been amusing, and he had served her purpose.

9

THE ARMADA

WITH THE dismissal of Anjou, Elizabeth's subjects were forced to confront the fact that she never was going to marry and provide them with an heir. There was no point in telling themselves that she was merely being wilful, that she would see sense and settle down with some husband, any husband, as long as he was not a foreign king or an ambitious Englishman. They realised at last that they were ruled by an ageing spinster, and they would have to make the best of it.

Moreover, after all her dalliance with Roman Catholic suitors they could hardly keep on hailing her as Deborah, the protector of Protestantism, especially as she was so open in her condemnation of her most Protestant subjects. The growing number of English Puritans disliked the episcopal form of church government and wanted to replace bishops with a series of church courts. The Queen would have none of it. Young James VI of Scotland might stomach his preachers telling him that he was only a subject of God like everyone else, but she was Supreme Governor of the Church of England and however much she might despise her bishops she firmly believed that they were necessary for the peace and order of her realm.

When, just a month after Anjou's death, William of Orange was assassinated and the Dutch offered her the sovereignty of their country in return for her protection, she refused point blank. She would not dream of accepting the allegiance of another monarch's people, she said. However, Burghley and Leicester insisted that England would be in deadly danger if Spain regained

121. *Sir Philip Sidney*, Leicester's nephew, who died of a wound received at Zutphen. This is an eighteenth-century copy of an earlier portrait.
(National Portrait Gallery, London)

complete control of the Netherlands and so she reconsidered. She signed the Treaty of Nonsuch, promising the Dutch 4000 foot soldiers and 400 horse. When the Spaniards captured Antwerp, she dispatched Leicester's nephew, Sir Philip Sidney, with additional men to garrison Flushing.

Leicester himself had been so loud in his demands that she should send assistance because he had identified a marvellous opportunity to win military glory for himself before it was too late. He was just over fifty and he had not fought in battle for nearly thirty years, but he was determined to go to the Netherlands as Elizabeth's commander-in-chief. She did not want him to risk his life for these wretched Dutch Calvinists, but in the end she gave way and on 6 December 1585 he sailed from Harwich with strict orders to have nothing to do with any offers of Dutch sovereignty.

Arriving on the other side, he was given such a hero's welcome that when the Dutch offered to make him Governor of the Netherlands, he accepted. He knew very well that Elizabeth would not be pleased, so he did not tell her. Instead, he waited until he had been safely installed, and then he dispatched a letter of explanation to her, instructing William Davison, his messenger, to take as long as possible on the way.

Rumours travelled faster than official communications, of course, and when Davison arrived in London he found Elizabeth in a fury. She had learned that Leicester was being addressed as 'Your Excellency', that he was being treated like a prince and that his wife Lettice was assembling a veritable court of ladies preparatory to joining him. This last piece of gossip was untrue, but as far as the Queen was concerned it was the final insult. When Davison was ushered into her presence she would not let him speak at all, and when her councillors finally persuaded her to listen to what he had to say, she constantly interrupted his stammering recital with exclamations of disbelief and scathing comments. When he attempted to hand her Leicester's letter, she waved it away.

He tried again the following day, and this time she did take it from him. She was thrown into a worse fury than ever when she read it and she immediately composed a letter of stinging rebuke in reply. 'We could never have imagined had we not seen it fall out in experience', she said, 'that a man raised up by ourself, and extraordinarily favoured by us above any other subject of this land, would have in so contemptible a sort have broken our commandment in a cause that so greatly toucheth us in honour.' He was to obey the bearer's instructions immediately, 'whereof fail you not, as you will answer the contrary at your utmost peril'.

These instructions were that he was to resign office at once, in public, in the very place where he had accepted it. It would be a dreadful humiliation. Her Privy Councillors were deeply shocked and they pleaded with her not to go ahead. She ignored them until Burghley played his usual trump card and threatened to resign. She then agreed to modify her commands. She would not insist that the resignation be in public.

Fully apprised of her frightening reaction, Leicester fell back on his usual procedure when he had annoyed her. He wrote her a grovelling letter of apology and sent word that he was ill. She never could resist that. In an instant, she was full of concern for him, talking once more about her 'sweet Robin' and saying that it had all been a misunderstanding. She had merely been annoyed at not being kept informed of what he was doing.

He would have to give up office, of course, but not until he came home again. 'We are persuaded that you, that have so long known us, cannot think

that ever we could have been drawn to take up so hard a course herein, had we not been provoked by an extraordinary cause', she wrote in her next letter to him. 'But that for your grieved and wounded mind hath more need of comfort than reproof . . . we think meet to forbear to dwell upon a matter wherein we ourselves do find so little comfort, assuring you that whosoever professeth to love you best taketh not more comfort for your well-doing, or discomfort of your evil-doing, than ourself.'

124. *Mary, Queen of Scots* during her captivity in England, a miniature by Hilliard. (By courtesy of the Board of Trustees of the Victoria and Albert Museum)

125. *Sir Francis Walsingham*, Elizabeth's Secretary of State, probably painted by J de Critz. (National Portrait Gallery, London)

His lacerated pride had been soothed, but the damage to his campaign was irreparable. The very public differences between the Queen and her commander had undermined the confidence of the Dutch, the money she sent was not nearly enough and his allies found Leicester impossibly rude and overbearing. His popular nephew Sir Philip Sidney died of a wound received at the siege of Zutphen, he himself achieved little, and there was relief all round when he sailed for home in November 1586, in time to give Elizabeth his advice in the latest crisis.

Ever since the Ridolfi Plot, Mary, Queen of Scots had been at the centre of one conspiracy after another, each more dangerous than the last. For years Elizabeth had kept on negotiating with the royal prisoner, some said in a genuine attempt to find a means of restoring her, others, from a cynical desire to satisfy her own continential allies. Parliament and in particular the Puritans were becoming increasingly vociferous in their demands for her execution but Elizabeth continued to frustrate any legislation aimed at beheading the Scottish Queen or removing her from the succession.

By the late 1580s, Burghley and his friends had reached the conclusion that they would never persuade her to execute Mary unless she were frightened into doing so. Her Secretary of State, Sir Francis Walsingham, therefore initiated a series of elaborate conspiracies designed to ensnare Mary. The Babington Plot of 1587 was not the first, but it was the most successful. Walsingham's spies were all around the Queen of Scots, he lured her into a secret correspondence with Sir Anthony Babington, who was plotting to assassinate Elizabeth, and then he intercepted her letters. In case these were not incriminating enough, he forged a postscript to one of them, giving the impression that Mary was asking for details of the men who would kill the Queen of England.

As he had foreseen, Elizabeth was thrown into a panic. She demanded a slow and lingering death for Babington and his fellow-conspirators, but even then she drew back from the idea of prosecuting Mary. Burghley and the Privy Council gave her solemn warning that unless she did so, there would be no end to the assassination plots and the next might be successful. She saw the truth of that, and she agreed that Mary shoud be tried. However, her councillors were worried and her secretary William Davison told Walsingham that she 'will keep the course she held with the Duke of Norfolk, which is not to take her life without extreme fear compel her'.

The trial opened at Fotheringhay Castle on 15 October 1587. Forty-two commissioners, including Burghley and Leicester, had ridden down from London and Mary appeared before them, clad in black, heavy, middle-aged and lame from rheumatism but as proud and as dignified as ever. She denied that she had ever plotted Elizabeth's death and she refused to recognise the jurisdiction of the court. She was a Queen: no one had a right to try her. At twelve o'clock that night, Elizabeth told Davison that the commissioners must not pronounce sentence, and so the following day the Lord Chancellor closed the proceedings and they all rode back to London.

There then followed a strange, uneasy interlude. The Privy Council tried in vain to persuade Elizabeth to allow the commissioners to pass sentence, and she insisted on postponing the next session of parliament because she knew that the members would put even more pressure on her. Even so, when the special French ambassador, the Sieur de la Mauvissière, came to her on 23 October to plead for Mary's life, she told him bluntly that it was too late to stop the proceedings now. A few hours later, she ordered the commissioners to pronounce their sentence.

They assembled in the Star Chamber on 25 October to announce that Mary was guilty. They did not have the power to impose the death sentence, but the Privy Council was able to proceed under the 1585 Act of Association which had authorised the execution of any who plotted against Elizabeth's life. The sentence could not be carried out, however, until she herself issued a proclamation naming the guilty person.

At first, she did nothing, just as they had feared. She stayed at Richmond instead of moving to Whitehall when parliament assembled on 29 October and when a deputation from the Lords and Commons went to her there, demanding Mary's death, she thanked them for their loyal concern and said she would send them her answer. They waited impatiently, but no answer came. Three days later they rode back again and Elizabeth saw them once more. The speech she made them was one of her masterpieces of evasion: 'If I should say I would not do what you request, it might peradventure be more than I thought, and to say I would do it might perhaps breed peril of that you labour to preserve, being more than in your own wisdoms and discretions would seem convenient, circumstances of place and time being duly considered . . . And thus I must deliver you an answer, answerless . . .'

She was more open with the French ambassador. When he went to her again to plead for the Scottish Queen she told him tersely that 'This justice was being done on a bad woman protected by bad men', and she went on to say that Mary must die if Elizabeth were to live, or Elizabeth must die if Mary were to survive. As had happened so many times before, her maddening procrastination was only superficial. At the back of her mind, she knew what she must do. The delays were partly an attempt to accustom Mary's allies to the idea that she must die, partly a necessary interval to allow Elizabeth to nerve herself to do something which she found instinctively distasteful.

She told Burghley that she would prorogue parliament, she changed her mind next morning and said she would adjourn it instead, she seemed deaf to her councillors' persuasions but on 1 December she signed the proclamation Burghley had drafted naming Mary as one who had plotted against her life. It was published on 4 December amidst wild rejoicings. Now all that remained was for her to sign the death warrant. She paced her apartments restlessly, muttering over and over again, in Latin, 'Suffer or strike, strike or be struck'. According to the resident French ambassador, Monsieur de l'Aubespine, Leicester and Walsingham were constantly with her, urging her to order Mary's death, but still she did nothing. Finally, they frightened her into action. At the end of January, they revealed to her the details of another assassination plot, telling her that the French ambassador was implicated. As long as Mary was alive, Elizabeth would never be safe.

On 1 February her secretary William Davison came to her with a pile of papers and she signed each one with scarcely a glance. She would say afterwards that she had no idea he had concealed the fatal warrant among them, but she knew. When she handed it back to him she could not resist remarking that he must tell Walsingham that it was signed at last. Sir Francis was ill at home and, she said sarcastically, 'the grief thereof would go near to kill him'.

As Davison was about to leave the room, she called him back. It would be far better, she said, if he could arrange for someone to murder Mary quietly. She was not alone in this opinion. Leicester had all along urged the use of poison and even Archbishop Whitgift had said that Elizabeth's reputation would be protected if Mary were eliminated secretly. Sir Amyas Paulet, the stern Puritan gentleman in charge of the royal prisoner at Fotheringhay, took a different view. When Elizabeth's suggestion was put to him, he exclaimed indignantly, 'God forbid that I should make so foul a shipwreck of my conscience!'

Mary, Queen of Scots went to the block on 8 February 1587, declaring that she died a martyr for her Roman Catholic faith. News of her execution did not reach court until the following day. Elizabeth was told when she arrived back from her morning ride, and she betrayed no emotion. Two days later, when her faithful admirer Sir Christopher Hatton arrived to see her, she seemed to be beside herself with rage, screaming that she had never meant the warrant to be used. Davison had been far too quick in sending it off. He had betrayed her.

The following day she ranted and raved at her council, declaring that she would execute Davison for his officiousness. Appalled, Burghley and the others went on their knees and pleaded with her to pause for thought. The man had done no wrong. He was certainly not guilty of a treasonable crime. They could not stop her from sending him to the Tower, however, and although in the end he was released, his career was in ruins.

After venting her wrath on the council, Elizabeth wrote to James VI. He was a grown man of twenty, and he might take reprisals against her. She swore to him that she had been utterly astonished to hear of his mother's death. The news had thrown her into such grief of mind and unfeigned weeping as she had never before experienced, she said. Desperately anxious to inherit her throne, James made only a formal protest and privately sent word to her that he did not blame her. It had all been her Privy Council's fault, he felt sure. She was greatly relieved. As for the French, they rioted in the streets, putting up black-draped portraits of Mary and screaming for

126. *The Execution of Mary, Queen of Scots* drawn by a Dutch artist.
(Scottish National Portrait Gallery)

vengeance, but although Henry III and Catherine de Medici broke with tradition to attend the memorial service in person, incognito, there was no danger that they would take any other action.

The real threat came from Spain. Putting on mourning, Philip II went to a special Requiem Mass and wrote sombrely to a friend, 'I have been deeply hurt by the death of the Queen of Scots . . . It is very fine for the Queen of England now to want to give out that it was done without her wish, the

128. *Philip II of Spain* by S Coello.
(The Prado, Madrid)

127. *Sir Christopher Hatton*, devoted admirer of Elizabeth, and her Lord Chancellor, painted about 1590 by an unknown artist.
(National Portrait Gallery, London)

129. *Sir Francis Drake*, 1581, seen in a miniature perhaps from the studio of Nicholas Hilliard.
(National Portrait Gallery, London)

130. *Alexander Farnese, Duke of Parma*, nephew of Philip II and his Governor of the Netherlands, painted by Otto van Veen.
(Musées Royaux des Beaux-Arts de Belgique, Brussels)

131. *Charles, Lord Howard of Effingham*, Lord Admiral and commander-in-chief against the Armada, painted by Daniel Mytens.
(The Trustees of the National Maritime Museum)

125

contrary being so clearly the case'. He spoke of his willingness to join France in a crusade against England should the Pope call for one, and his own confessor was constantly reminding him that he had a moral obligation to avenge Mary's death. Not long before, she had sent him word that she was bequeathing to him her claim to the throne of England, since her own son was a heretic. Now he would take up that claim, not on his own behalf, but for his beloved daughter the Infanta Isabella.

For years the Spaniards had been infuriated by Elizabeth's attacks on their trade with the New World. Instead of respecting the Pope's division of the Americas between Spain and Portugal, she had tacitly encouraged her privateers like Francis Drake and John Hawkins to intercept Philip's treasure ships and burn his settlements. As if that were not bad enough, there was her perpetual meddling in the Netherlands and her assistance to the rebels there. His patience had eventually run out, and for the past three years he had been equipping a vast fleet which he meant to send against England, in conjunction with an army of invasion from his forces in the Netherlands.

When she first heard reports of his naval preparations, Elizabeth refused to believe them. Convinced at last that he was making ready for war, she opened negotiations with his nephew the Duke of Parma, Regent of the Netherlands, and finally she gave in to Drake's pleas to be allowed to attack the gathering Armada in its own port. On 2 April 1587 he sailed from Plymouth in the *Elizabeth Bonaventura* to set fire to the vessels assembled in the harbour at Cadiz. Having successfully 'singed the King of Spain's beard', he intercepted Philip's East India fleet and arrived back in England with £40,000 for Elizabeth and another £17,000 for himself.

The Armada was unable to sail that summer, but everyone knew that it was only a matter of time before the enemy ships were sighted in the Channel. That winter passed and nothing happened. Spring came and there was no news, but finally, in June, there were reports which were both alarming and encouraging. In May the Armada had finally sailed from Lisbon, only to be scattered by tremendous gales a few days later at Corunna.

Drake was all for setting out at once to finish the work the storm had begun, but Elizabeth would not allow it. She was still negotiating with Parma and she was also afraid of England being left unprotected. The Spaniards might slip past Drake and that would have disastrous consequences. She hesitated and delayed, until even the cautious Lord Howard of Effingham, her Lord Admiral, was urging her to act. 'For the love of Jesus Christ, Madam', he wrote to her on 23 June, 'awake thoroughly and see the villainous treasons about you, against Your Majesty and your realm, and draw your forces round about you, like a mighty Prince, to defend you. Truly, Madam, if you do so there is no cause to fear.' In the end, she allowed her ships to go, but by the time they sailed into the Bay of Biscay the winds had veered round to the south and they were driven back again to Plymouth.

Elizabeth was at Richmond and Sir Francis Drake was playing bowls on Plymouth Hoe when the Armada was sighted off the Lizard on 19 July. 'We have time to finish the game and beat the Spaniards too', said Drake with merry sang-froid. He knew that he could not sail until nightfall. By then, the tide was right, and the English ships began to slip out of the harbour as flames from the warning beacons all round the coast leaped into the darkening sky. The following morning, the Armada was plainly visible from the land, 130 vessels in all, carrying over 30,000 men, nearly 20,000 of them soldiers, along with sailors, gunners, servants, medical staff, clerks and priests.

This was a holy war, they had been told. Their Admiral, the Duke of Medina Sidonia, was flying a standard blessed for him in Lisbon Cathedral. On one side was an image of the Virgin, on the other, Philip II's arms and the crucified Christ. A scroll read, 'Arise, O Lord, and Vindicate Thy Cause'. The Duke had issued careful instructions to his men, forbidding swearing, gambling and all unseemly behaviour, but encouraging them with the assurance that they would arrive in England to find waiting to assist them not only all the English martyrs and saints from time past but 'The blessed and innocent Mary, Queen of Scotland who, still fresh from her sacrifice, bears copious and abundant witness to the cruelty and impiety of this Elizabeth, and directs her shafts against her . . .'.

The wind was blowing from the west and, ahead of the English, the Armada sailed steadily up the Channel. No one had ever seen a fleet of such terrifying magnitude before. The great galleons were tall, heavy and slow to manoeuvre, yet even as the English watched they took up their famous battle formation, packed closely together in a crescent, most of the ships in the centre. That made it extremely difficult to attack and Howard knew that, outnumbered as he was, he would have to rely on the speed of his lighter, faster vessels and move against the tips of the crescent. Sending out his own personal pinnace to the Duke of Medina Sidonia with a formal challenge, he ordered his ships into single file and set off against the northernmost wing of the crescent.

It was the first of a series of running battles. The English tried in vain to slip past the Armada on the landward side, but it was impossible, so instead they fired on stragglers, always keeping out of their reach. The Spanish idea of naval warfare was to throw grappling irons on to the enemy ships, draw them in close and then fight what amounted to a land battle on the decks. The English dared not risk that, and with their bigger, faster-firing guns, they concentrated on keeping the Spanish at a distance.

On the evening of Wednesday, 3 August, the wind dropped and as the two fleets drifted within sight of each other, Howard called a council of war. It was decided to divide the English ships into four squadrons, one led by Howard himself, one by Drake, one by Hawkins and the other by Martin Frobisher. When the wind filled their sails once more, they moved on, attacking the stragglers even more effectively than before.

Late in the evening of Saturday, 6 August the Armada reached Calais and both fleets dropped anchor once more, just a long culverin shot away from one another. The Duke of Medina Sidonia had been expecting at any moment to see his ally Parma's army emerge on barges from the mouth of the River Sluys, but the seas ahead remained puzzlingly empty. Because of overwhelming transport difficulties and the fact that the Dutch were patrolling the coast, Parma was unable to set out for his rendezvous.

That same night, Howard's council of war decided to send fire ships against the enemy. The weather was perfect for it, the element of surprise was all-important, and the sudden appearance of burning vessels would inevitably cause terror and confusion. Eight large ships were packed with inflammable material and made ready, their guns primed to go off in the heat. The signal was given, they were set alight and then they were towed towards the enemy and cut loose.

When Medina Sidonia saw the flames he took immediate action, ordering a group of pinnaces and ships' boats to stand guard to the west of his fleet, with the intention of intercepting the fire ships and towing them away. The blazing vessels were too big for them, and they managed to seize only two

132. Detail of painting showing the Duke of Medina Sidonia (right) with Admiral Perez de Guzman, by Eugenio Caxes.
(The Prado, Madrid)

133. *English Ships and the Spanish Armada, August 1588,* by an unknown English artist of the sixteenth century. (The Trustees of the National Maritime Museum)

of the eight. The others went sailing into the midst of the fleet and the Spaniards panicked, their ships colliding with each other as they tried to move away, their sails catching light. In the chaos, Howard attacked, and the last, decisive fight took place off Gravelines.

Somehow, Medina Sidonia managed to get his fleet back into its crescent, and the battle raged from soon after dawn until four in the afternoon. Just when it seemed that the shattered Armada would perish on the Flanders Sands, a sudden violent squall sent the galleons further north, out of range of the English guns, and Howard watched in admiring disbelief as the survivors once more took up their crescent shape, ready to fight on. He had almost no ammunition left, so he could not attack again. Instead, he followed the Armada as it was blown northwards, past Hull, past Newcastle, past Berwick. Only when he finally saw the Spanish vessels making for the Firth of Forth did he know that the danger was past, and he turned and sailed for the south.

While the Duke of Medina Sidonia led the remains of his fleet the long way home, through dreadful storms, round the north coast of Scotland and south again by Ireland, Elizabeth and her army waited, expecting at any moment to hear that Parma was on his way from the Netherlands. Everyone had been impressed with the Queen's resolute behaviour during the crisis. 'It is a comfort', said Burghley's son Robert, 'to see how great magnanimity Her Majesty shows, who is not a whit dismayed', and she decided to rally her troops in person.

Leicester was in command of more than 4000 men at Tilbury, and on 18 August the Queen travelled by barge from St James's Palace to visit his camp. She had dressed with her usual care for the occasion, putting a silver cuirass with a mythological design over her white velvet dress. In her right hand she carried a commander's silver truncheon and she rode on a white gelding. In

134. Gold cross recovered from the
Girona, one of the Armada vessels
wrecked off the coast of Ireland. It
belonged to one of the knights of the
Order of St John, probably to the ship's
captain, Fabricio Spinola.
(The Ulster Museum, Belfast)

135. The Armada Jewel, given by
Elizabeth to Sir Thomas Heneage to
commemorate the defeat of the Armada.
(By courtesy of the Board of Trustees of
the Victoria and Albert Museum)

front of her walked two pages in white velvet. One was leading her horse, while the other carried her ornate silver helmet on a white velvet cushion. On her right rode the Earl of Leicester, on her left the Earl's handsome young stepson, Robert, Earl of Essex.

She inspected the camp and all the soldiers, and the next day, after a review and a march past, she decided to address her men. People had warned her against trusting herself to the armed multitudes for fear of treachery, she told them,

> but I assure you, I do not desire to live to distrust my faithful and loving people. Let tyrants fear. I have always so behaved myself that, under God, I have placed my chiefest strength and safeguard in the loyal hearts and good will of my subjects, and therefore I am come amongst you, as you see, at this time, not for my recreation and disport, but being resolved in the midst and heat of the battle to live or die amongst you all, to lay down for my God and for my kingdom and for my people, my honour and my blood, even in the dust. I know I have the body of a weak and feeble woman, but I have the heart and stomach of a king, and of a king of England too, and think foul scorn that Parma or Spain or any prince of Europe should dare invade the borders of my realm, to which, rather than any dishonour shall grow by me, I myself will take up arms . . .

Amidst rousing cheers, she went to dine with Leicester in his tent, and all the captains came to kiss her hand. The following day, as she sat at dinner with him, word arrived that Parma was about to set sail. She was all for staying to confront him in person, but her anxious ministers hurried her back to the greater safety of St James's.

In the event, the rumour proved to have been false, but everyone was most impressed with her courage. 'Nor has the Queen . . . lost her presence of

136. *Elizabeth I* in the dress she wore to attend the thanksgiving for victory over the Armada; drawn by an unknown artist. (Windsor Castle, Royal Library. © 1990 Her Majesty The Queen)

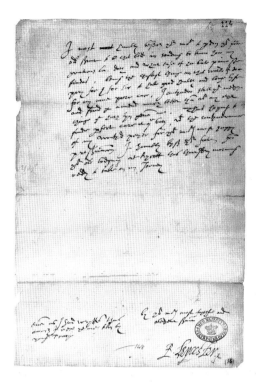

137. The Earl of Leicester's last
letter to Elizabeth.
(Public Record Office, London)

mind for a single moment', the Venetian ambassador in Paris reported to the
Doge, 'nor neglected aught that was necessary for the occasion. Her acuteness
in resolving on her action, her courage in carrying it out, show her high-
spirited desire of glory and her resolve to save her country and herself.'

As the days went by, it became evident that England was indeed safe.
Parma never would come, many of the great ships of the Armada had been
lost and the whole enterprise was in ruins. The Duke of Medina Sidonia did
manage to get back to Spain with the remnants of his fleet, but all his surviving
commanders soon died of fever and exhaustion and he himself lay ill for
many months afterwards. In England, sailors were dying in the streets of the
Channel ports from sickness and starvation. Elizabeth went to a service of
thanksgiving in St Paul's Cathedral on 24 November but in spite of her promises at Tilbury of just rewards she had failed to authorise payment of her
navy's wages and the purchase of their stores.

Death also took her dearest friend. The Earl of Leicester had worked tire-
lessly at Tilbury, organising her army and her camp, but he had long been
suffering from a recurrent fever. Tired and weak, he set out in September
with Lettice for Buxton, meaning to take the waters, but he died on the way.
He was fifty-five. In his will he left Elizabeth a jewel of emeralds and diamonds
and a rope of 600 pearls. He owed her thousands of pounds, however, and
she insisted that his widow sell his personal effects to repay the debt. She
never could forgive Lettice for having married him. Apparently unconcerned
by her hostility, Lady Leicester took a third husband and lived to the age of
ninety-two.

Elizabeth's feelings for Robert remained unchanged, and for the rest of her
life she kept in a cabinet by her bedside a small, crumpled piece of paper. On
the outside she had written, 'His last letter'. These few words were a more
eloquent testimony to the depth of her feelings than any elaborate elegy could
have been.

10

GLORIANA

WITH THE the defeat of the Armada, Elizabeth was triumphant. Anne Boleyn's precocious child, the tremulous girl confronting Mary Tudor, the excitable flirt risking her reputation with Leicester and the shrill termagant storming at her ministers were all forgotten in that moment of victory. Now she was truly 'Fair Cynthia, the wide Ocean's Empress', the epitome of all the virtues. She was in her fifties. She had put on weight, her dresses had been let out, her hair was thinning, her teeth decaying, her fine fair skin beginning to wrinkle, but she pinned on her extravagant red wigs, painted her face, stuffed fine cloths into her cheeks to prevent them from looking too sunken, and danced and hunted and joked and teased as she had always done, while her courtiers responded with their polished compliments and their poems of praise.

Flirting was safer now. When she was in her twenties, there had always been the danger that some man might take her at her word, think that she

138. *George Clifford, 3rd Earl of Cumberland*, shown as Queen's Champion at The Tilt, in a Hilliard miniature of about 1590.
(The Trustees of the National Maritime Museum)

139. *Elizabeth I* by or after George Gower, painted to commemorate the defeat of the Armada.
(National Portrait Gallery, London)

wanted him in her bed. She had kept them at a distance with her sharp tongue, forced them to play the game of courtly love, recognise that she was the untouchable lady and they the humble knights who must adore from a distance. As time passed, although they still used the language of sexual attraction, both she and they knew very well that this was a convention, a means of making it acceptable for proud, energetic men to accept the orders of a woman, and an ageing woman at that.

When she had first come to the throne at twenty-five, she had been younger than all her ministers and most of her courtiers. They had been so relieved at being ruled by a Protestant monarch that they had submitted to her, and they had spoken to her with fatherly kindness mingled with respect because she

140. *Henry IV of France* by an unknown artist.
(Bibliothèque Nationale, Paris)

141. *Elizabeth Vernon, Countess of Southampton*, one of Elizabeth's young maids of honour, by an unknown artist.
(The Duke of Buccleuch and Queensberry KT)

was King Harry's daughter. She allowed them to compare her to Old Testament heroines, for all her own loathing of theological debate, nor did she utter any criticism when some began to call her the Virgin Queen. She had been born on the feast of the Nativity of the Virgin Mary, they remembered, and if they drew strange, near-blasphemous comparisons it did not disturb her. After all, in the wake of the Reformation, her subjects missed the feasts and festivals of the old religion. They needed something to celebrate instead, and by the 1570s she was permitting celebrations of her own accession day with lavish tournaments devised by Sir Henry Lee.

Time passed, and so many of those she knew were gone. In July 1589 Henry III of France was murdered by a Jacobin monk and his energetic, determined Protestant brother-in-law Henry of Navarre succeeded him. In 1598 Lord Burghley fell gravely ill. She sent him kind messages and she visited him, even feeding him with her own hand as he lay propped on his pillows, but he was old and nothing could be done to help him. He died, and she felt dreadfully alone. She could never hear his name mentioned, after that, without the tears coming to her eyes. She had promised him that she would let his son Robert succeed him, but although the little hunchback was astute and diligent he would never be the man his father was. A few months after Burghley's death, Philip II succumbed to a long and trying illness. His young son Philip III would rule Spain in his place, while his daughter the Infanta Isabella governed the Netherlands. The whole world was changing.

It was a consolation when poets praised her as Judith, Diana, Gloriana and Belphoebe. In her day no one had to consult a dictionary to discover which qualities these biblical or mythological figures possessed. The allusions to other notable virgins were equally recognisable and Elizabeth, that least sentimental of women, was well content that her subjects thought of her in such flattering terms. Ever the realist, she was well aware that she was older, now, than many of her statesmen and her nobility, that she was surrounded by eager young men who might have been all too ready to rebel against a solitary spinster had she not come to personify their own victorious England. Reassuring the rhetoric might be, but she inhabited the real world, not some fabled realm, and she had to battle with the painful problems of loneliness, isolation, ingratitude and betrayal, never more so, perhaps, than in her relationship with her latest protégé Robert Devereux, Earl of Essex.

It was strange that she was so fond of him, for he was Lettice's son, the child of the woman she always called 'the she-wolf'. He was only eight years old when his father died in Ireland, leaving him in the care of Lord Burghley. That was when Elizabeth first saw him. He was brought to her one day, a thin, delicate, pretty child with dark curly hair and large dark eyes. He was shy. He hung his head bashfully when she spoke to him and when she bent to kiss him he backed nervously away.

He was a clever boy, fond of his books, and he was sent to Cambridge at the early age customary in his day. He was eleven when his mother married Leicester, and he did not like the ebullient, overpowering Earl. When he was sixteen, his stepfather summoned him to court. He did not want to go and for a time he refused, but no one could defy Lord Leicester indefinitely and in the end he rode to London to be presented again to the Queen.

His relationship with his stepfather improved after that, and he set off with him as General of the Horse when Leicester went on his ill-fated expedition to the Netherlands. It was when they returned at the end of 1586 that Elizabeth really began to take notice of him. He had grown into a tall, handsome, graceful young man with a quiet, courteous manner. Whenever she was feeling bored she would send for him and soon he was occupying the difficult role of royal favourite, spending hours in her company, dealing with tiresome courtiers and petitioners. She made him her Master of Horse, teased him and laughed when he was jealous of her friend Sir Walter Raleigh or of Lord Burghley's son Robert.

After a few years, he became restless. The bashful, bookish boy had grown into a vigorous, ambitious man, eager for military honours and political power. The Queen was too possessive. She wanted him always on hand, ready to dance attendance on her day and night. With Leicester gone, he was more precious to her than ever, a cherished link with his stepfather. Her feelings for him were not those of a woman towards her lover. He was more the son she and the Earl never had.

He began to long for freedom, adventure, the opportunity to prove himself. Desperate to get away from the stifling atmosphere of the court, he slipped off to join Drake's expedition to put the pretender, Don Antonio, on the throne of Portugal. Elizabeth was furious when she found out that he had gone. No one had the right to leave court without permission, least of all him. Terrified that some harm would befall him, she ordered Drake to send him back at once. Contrary winds prevented him from coming and so she fired off another angry letter, commanding Drake to obey. 'If ye do not, ye shall look to answer at your smart!' she warned. Essex returned, and although she gave him a chilly reception, he was soon as high in her favour as before.

It seemed both to himself and to his jealous rivals that he would always be able to win her round. He even managed to make a secret marriage with Sir Philip Sidney's widow without being sent to the Tower, and from time to

142. *Elizabeth I* standing on Oxfordshire, near Sir Thomas Lee's house of Ditchley. This portrait, by Marcus Gheeraerts the Younger, was the largest ever painted of the Queen.
(National Portrait Gallery, London)

time Elizabeth agreed to let him go off on military expeditions, although she worried constantly about his safety. In 1591 he was in France, helping the new King Henry IV, and a few years after that he scored a brilliant success when he captured Cadiz from the Spanish. He was a member of the Privy Council by now, and he was recognised as leader of the war party, urging military action against Spain and continually criticising the policies of the English commanders in Ireland.

Ever since the beginning of her reign, Elizabeth had been trying without success to force the Roman Catholic Irish to accept English Protestant rule. They remained in a continual state of rebellion and her Privy Council were at a loss to find a solution to the problem. One day, when Essex was even more critical than usual of her administrators there, she told him sharply to keep his opinions to himself. In a shocking breach of court etiquette, he turned his back on her. Furious, she boxed him on the ear, telling him to go and be hanged. He was actually putting his hand on the hilt of his sword when the Lord Admiral stepped quickly between them. Essex flung away and left the court, while his colleagues shook their heads and muttered to each other that something would have to be done. The favourite was becoming far too arrogant. One day he would go too far.

143. *Robert, Earl of Essex*, Elizabeth's favourite, in a miniature painted after 1596 by Isaac Oliver.
(National Portrait Gallery, London)

He regretted his rashness himself in 1599 when the post of Lord Deputy in Ireland was vacant and the council were discussing whom they should appoint. In his usual way, the Earl harangued them all about the deficiencies of the previous holders of the post, only to be told by Elizabeth that since he was so clever he could go and do the job himself. He was appalled. Nothing had been further from his intentions, but he could not refuse, and when he got there he began to understand why his predecessors had made so little progress. There was sickness in his army, there were far more rebels than he expected, supplies were difficult to obtain and his own council had to agree before he could make a move. Soon, the Queen was plying him with letters, telling him that he was wasting his time and her money. It seemed that he could do nothing right.

By the end of September he could stand it no longer. When he received yet another sharp letter, he lost his temper completely and he and his friend the Earl of Southampton spoke of raising an armed rebellion. Their horrified friend Sir Christopher Blount persuaded them not to do that, but Essex then had another disastrous idea. Elizabeth had expressly warned him not to come back to England without her permission. Ignoring this command, he set off to see her in person.

He sailed to England, rode hard for Nonsuch Palace and strode up to her bedchamber without even stopping to change his muddy clothes. She had just got up when he burst in unannounced, and she stood there astonished in the gown she wore in her bedchamber, her hair hanging wispily about her face. Her instinctive reaction was one of delight, however. She smiled, held out her hand to him and gave him a warm welcome. Her dear friend was safely by her side once more.

Later in the day, her attitude changed. She was gracious and friendly that afternoon but by evening, after her Privy Councillors had spoken to her, she sent Essex word that he was to remain in his chamber until the council sent for him. His conduct in Ireland had been extremely dubious, he was suspected of illicit dealings with the rebels and, worst of all, he had disobeyed the Queen's command.

The councillors questioned him the following day and then they had him arrested and sent to York House, the mansion of Lord Keeper Egerton. The Earl was already ill with dysentery and now he sank into a deep depression.

144. *Sir Walter Raleigh*, rival of Essex for Elizabeth's favour, in a Hilliard miniature of about 1585.
(National Portrait Gallery, London)

Elizabeth refused to see him, would not even let his wife visit him. His household was dispersed and his servants were sent away.

Weeks passed, and Essex's condition deteriorated. By December, he was sure that he was dying, and he sent the Queen a packet containing his patents as Master of the Horse and Master of the Ordnance, saying that he had no more need of them. That alarmed her. She sent them back at once, said his Countess might visit him and dispatched eight of her doctors to attend him. When they gave her their report, she listened to them with tears in her eyes, had a special broth prepared for him and even said she would go to see him herself. Nursed by his devoted wife, he began to recover, and he was further cheered by some news from Sir Robert Cecil. If he wrote the Queen a humble letter of apology, she would cancel his trial.

He wrote the letter, and in March she allowed him to go back to his own house, although he was to remain a prisoner there. His health improved, and he grew bored and resentful. On 5 June he was summoned to York House, where eighteen special commissioners were waiting to censure him. Throwing himself on his knees, he vowed his loyalty to the Queen and launched into a long, impassioned defence of his own actions. The Lord Keeper cut him short and told him that he was lucky. He was to continue under house arrest. If he had been tried in the Star Chamber, as had been Her Majesty's original intention, he would have been sentenced to life imprisonment and a heavy fine.

No one knew what would happen next, but in August Elizabeth announced that she was freeing him, although he was not to come to court. She fully intended to receive him back sooner or later, but she had been told that he was not quite humble enough yet. She longed to have him at her side again, but not while he was rebellious and troublesome. She would teach him one more lesson first. His most important source of revenue came from the sale of sweet wines. She was due to renew his licence that autumn, and if she did not do so he would be ruined financially. He wrote urgent letters to her about it: 'My soul cries out unto Your Majesty for grace, for access and for an end of this exile . . .'

He was sure that she would listen to his pleas, but he had reckoned without the fact that Elizabeth had never enjoyed an equal relationship with anyone. She had been, willingly or not so willingly, the humble subject of her father, her brother and her sister, and since then she had been the monarch, the source of all power. She was admired all over Europe for her shrewdness, her perspicacity, her understanding of human nature, but in her most intimate personal relationships she made no allowances for masculine dignity or pride. She had come to the brink of personal disaster before, when she wanted to humiliate Leicester publicly for accepting the governorship of the Netherlands. Her advisers had hastily intervened and that relationship was saved, but now there was no one to warn her of what might happen. Lord Burghley was gone and his son Robert had no great desire to assist his rival. On 30 October, Elizabeth let it be known that she would keep the revenues from the sweet wines in her own hands.

The fact that she did not grant them to someone else presumably meant that she intended restoring them to Essex eventually, but he was not to know that, nor did his friends realise it. Essex House became a gathering place for everyone who had a grudge: Puritans, Roman Catholics, people who objected to the government's fiscal policies, to monopolies and high taxation. The Earl of Southampton was always there and the Earls of Worcester, Sussex, Rutland

145. *King James VI of Scotland and I of England*, a miniature by Hilliard.
(By courtesy of the Board of Trustees of the Victoria and Albert Museum)

146. *Frances, Countess of Essex*, daughter of Sir Francis Walsingham, widow of Sir Philip Sidney and wife of Elizabeth's favourite, painted by Robert Peake the Elder in 1594 when she was thirty-six. The boy is Robert, son of Essex and herself.
(In a private collection)

and Bedford became regular visitors. At the centre of them all was Essex himself, mortified, resentful and obsessed.

He was taken up with public policy and with his own past insults. The Queen was still refusing to nominate her successor and he was desperately afraid that King James VI of Scotland was going to be passed over in favour of a Roman Catholic. The earls who rode down to see him brought all the latest rumours, and, according to one report, Robert Cecil wanted the Infanta Isabella to become Queen of England when Elizabeth died and was plotting to further the Spanish Princess's cause. Convinced that he must do something, Essex wrote secret letters to James to warn him of what was afoot. He received a reply which he refused to let anyone see. He placed it in a little leather bag, which he hung round his neck.

He listened with growing rage when people spoke to him about Ireland. The Queen had been completely unappreciative of his own efforts there. Now, she was full of praise for his successor, Lord Mountjoy. No nagging letters were sent to him. Instead, when Mountjoy, in a mood of depression, complained that he was being treated no better than a scullion, Elizabeth wrote to him jocularly in her own hand, addressing him as 'Mistress Kitchenmaid' and assuring him of her appreciation. The truth of the matter was that Elizabeth could afford to be generous to Mountjoy because her emotions were not involved, but that did not occur to Essex, and one day he burst out bitterly that Her Majesty's mind was as crooked as her carcase. He even spoke wildly of breaking into her apartments to seize her and govern in her name.

She got to hear of all this, of course, for her spy system was as efficient as ever, and Essex House was just a mile away from Whitehall. The Earls of

140

147. *Elizabeth I*, painted by Isaac Oliver about 1592. This was a pattern miniature, intended to be kept in his studio and copied every time a portrait was needed, hence the unfinished state of the dress and jewels.
(By courtesy of the Board of Trustees of the Victoria and Albert Museum)

Worcester, Sussex, Rutland and Bedford were arrested and the Privy Council summoned Essex himself to their presence. Twice he refused to go, and a deputation from the council rode down to Essex House, gained entrance and found themselves locked in on the Earl's orders, while he set off for Whitehall with a mob of followers, shouting 'For the Queen! For the Queen! A plot is laid for my life!'

Arriving at Sheriff Smyth's house he went in and waited confidently for the whole city of London to rise in his favour. No one came. At noon, Elizabeth sat down calmly to eat her dinner as though nothing were amiss. God had placed her in her seat as prince, she said, and he would preserve her in it. By two o'clock, Essex realised that it was no use. He set off for home, arrived back at Essex House after a brief skirmish on the way, and then he and his friends barricaded themselves in. When the Lord Admiral arrived with a small

141

force to seize him, he and a group of supporters emerged on to the roof, waving their swords and shouting defiance.

There were some shots, and eventually Lady Essex and the other women emerged, weeping. They were hurried away. Darkness fell, and it was ten o'clock at night before Essex and Southampton surrendered. They came down from the roof, out into the garden and knelt before the Lord Admiral by the light of flaring torches to hand over their swords. It was too late to take Essex to the Tower of London, which would be locked and barred for the night. Instead, he spent the night under guard in Lambeth Palace, and was escorted to the Tower the following morning.

He and Southampton were tried in Westminster Hall on 19 February 1601. Essex's former friend Sir Francis Bacon played a leading part in the prosecution, and in a dramatic intervention Robert Cecil came to give evidence. Strongly denying that he had ever said the Infanta should succeed to the throne of England, he declared that before all this had happened he would have pleaded with the Queen on his knees to spare Essex. Now, however, he told the Earl, 'You have a wolf's head in a sheep's garment, in appearance humble and religious, but in disposition ambitious and aspiring. God be thanked, we know you now'. Both prisoners were found guilty of treason and condemned to death.

Elizabeth had received regular reports of all that was going on. She remained convinced that Essex had been involved in treasonable dealings with the rebels in Ireland, but many of her courtiers believed that if the Earl pleaded for his life, she would save him. Time passed, and there was no message from him, only a report from the Privy Council that he had confessed everything.

148. *Robert Cecil*, who succeeded his father, Lord Burghley, as Elizabeth's chief minister, attributed to De Critz.
(National Portrait Gallery, London)

149. *Henry Wriothesley, 3rd Earl of Southampton*, painted by J de Critz during his imprisonment in the Tower, with his faithful cat which had joined him there. He was later released.
(The Duke of Buccleuch and Queensberry KT)

Elizabeth signed the death warrant. The two executioners arrived at the Tower on 24 February, but at the last moment the Queen told them to wait.

It was Shrove Tuesday, and there was the usual feasting at court to mark the beginning of Lent. Elizabeth attended the banquet and watched a performance by the Lord Chamberlain's players. Led by Richard Burbage, with William Shakespeare as their playwright, they usually performed at the Globe Theatre, built two years before, but they were always ready to come to court to entertain the Queen. She protected actors from the criticisms of the Puritans and she laughed loud and long at Shakespeare's comedies: *The Merry Wives of Windsor* was one of her favourites. That evening, the atmosphere was not so light-hearted but, even so, it was late when she retired to her apartments. Perhaps she still hoped that Essex would write to her, send a messenger, beg for his life. Nothing came, and that same night she gave orders for the execution to proceed. He was beheaded the next morning, protesting that he had never sought her death or intended violence against her. Elizabeth sat in her darkened chamber and wept.

By now, foreign ambassadors and, indeed, many of her own subjects were speculating in secret about how much longer she would reign. She was nearing seventy. She could not last much longer. Who would follow her? Surely she would choose her cousin's son, the Protestant James VI of Scotland, married now and with sons of his own. She kept up a regular correspondence with him, plying him with brisk advice, but in spite of all the clamouring of parliament she would not name her successor. Whenever they petitioned her about it she would give them vague, rambling replies, rebuking them for thinking that they could tell her what to do, that the feet could rule the head.

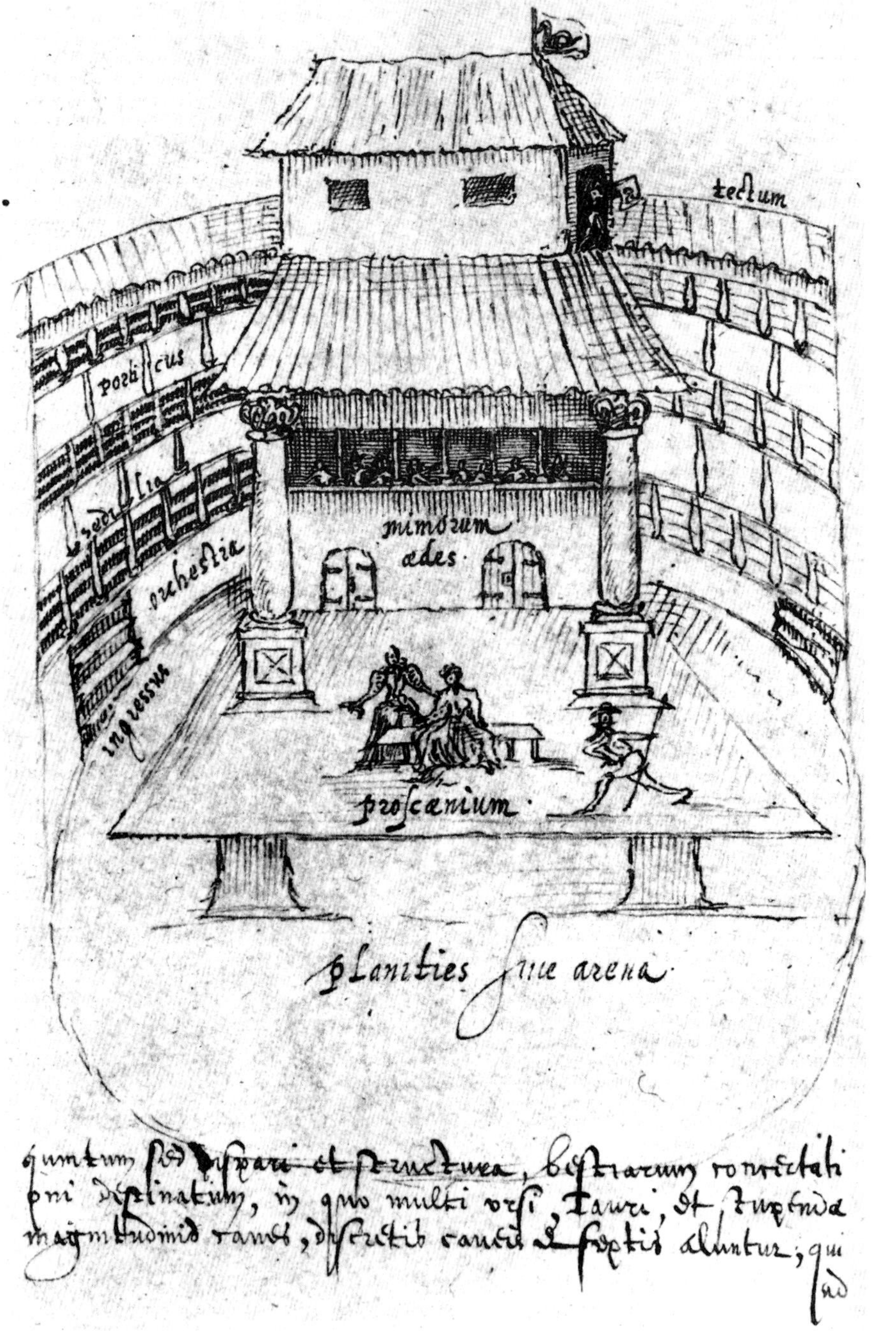
tectum
orchestra
mimorum
ædes
ingressus
proscænium
planities sive arena

150. The Swan Theatre, built on the south bank of the River Thames in 1594–5. This drawing by Jan de Witte is the only contemporary picture of the interior of an Elizabethan playhouse.
(The Mansell Collection)

She refused to contemplate the future. It did not interest her. She was still alive, still enjoying herself.

She lived on for another two years, as quick and sharp and determined as ever. In February 1603 the new Venetian Secretary in England, Giovanni Carlo Scaramelli, went to see her for the first time and he was impressed. He found

151. *Eliza Triumphans*, or *Elizabeth I going in procession to Blackfriars in 1600*, in the style of Peake.
(Private collection)

her in excellent health, he told the Doge and Senate, seated on a small platform, surrounded by her courtiers and 'clad in taffeta of silver and white, trimmed with gold, her dress somewhat open in front and showed her throat encircled with pearls and rubies down to her breast. Her skirts were much fuller and began lower down than is the fashion in France.

'Her hair was of a light colour, never made by nature, and she wore great pearls like pears round the forehead. She had a coif arched round her head and an Imperial crown, and displayed a vast quantity of gems and pearls upon her person. Even under her stomacher she was covered with golden jewelled girdles and single gems, carbuncles, balas-rubies, diamonds; round her wrists in place of bracelets she wore double rows of pearls of more than medium size.' She stood to speak to him, as she had always done, conversing graciously in Italian.

A month later, she was greatly changed. There had been talk of a new rebellion, a move to replace her with Arabella Stuart, Lady Lennox's grandchild. She seemed dreadfully depressed by the news. She did not leave her chamber for days, and when her coronation ring had to be sawn through and removed because it was cutting into her finger, she took it as a sinister omen. She had married England with that ring. Was their union about to end?

When the court moved to Richmond Palace, they all hoped she would recover her health but she caught a cold. She would hardly eat. She could not sleep at night and she refused to go to bed. Instead, she sat on her cushions in front of the fire, staring gloomily into the flames. When she did speak it was of Arabella, of Ireland and, most of all, of the Earl of Essex. She said she had found some letter amongst her papers proving him innocent of all the charges against him. He had not plotted against her with the Irish. He had been loyal, she now believed, and she had sent him to his death.

Her godson, Sir John Harrington, tried to cheer her up by telling her amus-

152. *Lady Arabella Stuart*, granddaughter of the Countess of Lennox and claimant of Elizabeth's throne, attributed to Peake.
(Scottish National Portrait Gallery)

ing stories, for he knew that she loved a joke. Instead of laughing uproariously she stared at him and said in sombre tones, 'When thou doth feel creeping time at thy gate, these fooleries will please thee less'. Sir Robert Cecil came to tell her that she must go to bed. 'The word "must" is not to be used to princes', she retorted, and then she added sadly, 'Little man, little man, if your father had lived you durst not had said so . . . but ye know that I must die, and that makes thee so presumptuous.'

At last, they did persuade her to lie down. 'I wish not to live any longer, but desire to die', she told her servants, and by 22 March they could see that the end was near. Her Privy Councillors gathered in her chamber, Sir Robert Cecil at the foot of the bed, the Lord Keeper on the left and the Lord Admiral on the right. There was one pressing problem in the forefront of all their minds and it was the Lord Admiral who finally plucked up the courage to put the vital question. Who was to be their next ruler? They bent closer to hear her reply, as she whispered, 'I tell you, my seat hath been the seat of kings. I will have no rascal to succeed me, and who should succeed me but a king?'

They gazed at each other, uncertain still, and then Cecil repeated the question. 'Who but our cousin of Scotland?' she murmured feebly, and then, 'I pray you, trouble me no more . . . I will have none but him . . .' Next day, she lay speechless, holding the hand of her faithful friend Archbishop Whitgift. After a muttered conclave with his colleagues, Cecil put his question to

153. *John Whitgift, Archbishop of Canterbury* by an unknown artist.
He and the Queen got on well together, all the more so because
he remained a bachelor.
(National Portrait Gallery, London)

her once more. They had to be absolutely sure. Could she give him a sign
that James VI really was her choice? She lay looking at them and then suddenly
she heaved herself up in bed, lifted her hands above her head and put her
fingers together in the form of a crown. They had their answer.

She died soon after midnight. Following a prearranged plan, one of her
ladies dropped a ring from the window to Sir Robert Carey, who was waiting
beneath. He set off at once for Edinburgh, to give King James VI of Scotland
the news that he was now King James I of England. Elizabeth's body was
embalmed and placed in a lead coffin. On 28 April 1603 her funeral procession
set out for Westminster Abbey, the Knight Marshal's men clearing a way
through the throng.

Almost everyone was there: Sir Robert Cecil, the Lord Mayor of London,
the French ambassador, the peers and the members of her household. Because
she was a female sovereign, 260 poor women walked in the procession, four
abreast, the chief mourner was the Marchioness of Northampton and all the
peeresses and the ladies of the court took part. The coffin, covered by a cloth
of purple velvet, was borne along on a chariot drawn by four horses with
black velvet trappings. Lying on the purple velvet, beneath a royal canopy,
was an effigy of the Queen in her parliament robes, a crown on her head and
a sceptre in her hand.

The Archbishop of Canterbury conducted the service, the choristers sang
and the congregation wept. Deborah, Judith, Cynthia and Gloriana, their

154. *Detail from* The Funeral of Queen Elizabeth, showing the effigy on her coffin. (The British Library)

Virgin Queen, their mighty Prince, was gone at last. For forty-five years she had ruled over them, infuriating them with her wilfulness, mystifying them with her constant changes of mind, but leading them to victory and international acclaim.

She had left them with all the problems she had so successfully ignored: the shortage of money, the unpopular fiscal measures, the rise of Puritanism and the demands of a discontented parliament. James, the son of their old enemy, Mary, Queen of Scots, was already on his way to London. Very soon, he would take his place as King of England and they would have to confront a whole new round of difficulties. However, as they buried her in the vault beside her sister Mary Tudor, they knew that she had left them a legacy of confidence and national pride which would endure for centuries to come.

155. The tomb of Queen Elizabeth I, erected in Westminster Abbey by her successor, King James VI and I.
(By courtesy of the Dean and Chapter of Westminster: photograph, A F Kersting)

FURTHER READING

FOR THOSE who wish to study Elizabeth's own writings, selections from her correspondence have been printed in *Letters of Queen Elizabeth* edited by G B Harrison (1935), *Letters of Queen Elizabeth and James VI* (1849) and, most recently, in Maria Perry, *Elizabeth I* (1990). Invaluable summaries of the reports of ambassadors and diplomats are to be found in *Calendar of Letters and State Papers relating to English Affairs preserved principally in the Archives of Simanacas, 1558–1603* edited by M A S Hume (1892–9), *Calendar of State Papers and Manuscripts relating to English Affairs in the Archives of Venice*, edited by Rawdon Brown and others (1864–1947), *Calendar of State Papers (Domestic Series) of the Reigns of Edward VI, Mary and Elizabeth (1547–1603)* edited by R Lemon and others (1856–70), and *Calendar of State Papers (Foreign Series) of the Reign of Elizabeth (1558–89)*, edited by J Stevenson and others (1863–1950). Correspondence of the French ambassadors is published in René de Vertot, *Ambassades de MM de Noailles en Angleterre* (1763), and S Haynes, *A Collection of State Papers left by William Cecil, Lord Burghley* (1740) is another useful source for contemporary material.

Hundreds of books have been written on the political, economic, religious and constitutional aspects of the period. It is possible to list only a few here. The lives of Elizabeth's parents may be followed in J J Scarisbrick, *Henry VIII* (1968) and Eric Ives, *Anne Boleyn* (1986). David Mathew, *Lady Jane Grey: The Setting of the Reign*, is a moving biography of the short-lived Queen. Elizabeth's childhood is documented in F A Mumby, *The Girlhood of Queen Elizabeth* (1909), the account for her clothing in 1535–6 is to be found in *Miscellania of the Philobiblon Society* vii (1862–3). Her household accounts for 1551–2 are printed in *Camden Miscellany* ii (1853).

Elizabeth's clothing in later years is detailed in Janet Arnold's encyclopaedic *The Secrets of Queen Elizabeth's Wardrobe Unlocked* (1987), and her portraits and image are discussed in Roy Strong's books, *The Cult of Elizabeth: Elizabethan portraiture and pageantry* (1977) and *Gloriana: The Portraits of Queen Elizabeth* (1987). Robin Headlam Wells considers the literary image-making in *Spenser's Faerie Queene and the Cult of Elizabeth* (1983) as does Elkin Calhoun Wilson in his classic *England's Eliza* (1939). A fascinating record of the Queen's travels and New Year gifts is preserved in John Nicols, *The Progresses and Public Processions of Queen Elizabeth* (1823).

Conyers Read discusses the role of Elizabeth's chief ministers in *Mr Secretary Cecil and Queen Elizabeth* (1955), *Lord Burghley and Queen Elizabeth* (1960) and *Mr Secretary Walsingham and the policy of Queen Elizabeth* (1925). Milton Waldman writes entertainingly on *Elizabeth and Leicester* (1944), G Mattingly recounts *The Defeat of the Spanish Armada* (1959) in vivid terms and Felipe Fernandez-Armesto gives the Spanish viewpoint in *The Spanish Armada* (1988). Alan Haynes, *The White Bear: the Elizabethan Earl of Leicester* (1987) and G B Harrison, *The Life and Death of Robert Devereux, Earl of Essex* (1937) outline the careers of the two favourites and Professor Ian Aird's article, 'The Death of Amy Robsart', was published in *English Historical Review*, lxxi (1956). Further details of the life of Mary, Queen of Scots are to be found in Rosalind K Marshall, *Queen of Scots* (HMSO 1986), the first biography in this present series.